BRAINS, BEAUTY, BOSS

Barloveujides

BRAINS, BEAUTY, BOSS

THE ULTIMATE GUIDE FOR WOMEN IN THE WORKPLACE

BARBARA EURIPIDES

NEW DEGREE PRESS

BRAINS, BEAUTY, BOSS

The Ultimate Guide for Women in the Workplace

ISBN   978-1-63676-513-6   *Paperback*

          978-1-63676-037-7   *Kindle Ebook*

          978-1-63676-038-4   *Ebook*

I dedicate this book to my mom, Joanne Euripides. Ever since the day I was born, my mom has taught me what it means to be a powerful, resilient woman in the workplace. From leading international STEM conferences weeks after giving birth, to patenting innovative chemical solutions in her twenties, my mom has defined what it truly means to be a trailblazer.

I am incredibly grateful to have been raised by a woman who champions female empowerment, standing up for what you believe in, and most importantly, standing up for yourself. I would not have the confidence I have today if it wasn't for my mom.

Mom, thank you for everything.

CONTENTS

—

ACKNOWLEDGMENTS

———

First and foremost, I'd like to thank my family. Mom, Dad, Elefteria, and Charlie, thank you for the constant love and support throughout this entire journey. You were all there for me from the day I "jokingly" brought up the idea I wanted to write a book, and you have been the most amazing support system since.

Theio John, Theia Voula, Yiorgo, and Yiayia, thank you for always being there for me, and for instilling confidence within me through each step of this journey.

Pappou, Uncle Richard, Theio Michael, Theia Evanthia, Aunt Mel, Theio Chris, Theia Sophia, Evan, Chrysanthi, Maria, and Evi, thank you for cheering me on and for always supporting me.

Theio George, thank you for mentoring me throughout this entire process.

Thank you to all of my interviewees from the *Forbes* 30 Under 30 list. Thank you for taking the time out of your busy schedules to speak with me about your pathways, and for sharing important advice that can help all women in the workplace.

Thank you to all of my friends from Duke to Myers Park, to Ionian Village, to everywhere in between. I'm forever grateful for your support, for promoting my book to everyone, and for always being there for me.

Lastly, thank you to the team at New Degree Press, especially Eric Koester, Brian Bies, Sarah Lobrot, and Margaret Danko, for helping me turn my childhood dream into a reality.

I would also like to acknowledge all of my beta readers and early supporters who helped me transform *Brains, Beauty, Boss* from an idea into a published book. I could not have done this without you.

Joanne Euripides	Ann Chanler
Charles Euripides	Eleni Navrosidis
Elefteria Euripides	Brina Melton
Charlie Euripides	Marisa Aleguas
John Maheras	Hayden Manseau
Bessie Maheras	Effie Ypsilantis
Maria Tassopoulos	Amanda Gavco
George Kroustalis	Victoria LePore
Vivian Diatzikis	Matthew Holcomb
Yiorgo Diatzikis	James Vounessea
Mel Gibson	Rebecca Erebaum
Evanthia and Michael Euripides	Katelyn Gallanty
	Kyra McDonald
Sophia and Chris Euripides	Victoria Sorhegui
George and Pitsa Diatzikis	Elizabeth Bartzokis
Phyllis Kaperonis	Amy Chen
Anna Maria Minakakis	Anna Moratis
Loula Minakakis	Montana Lee
Hannah Perkins	Christianna Brotsis
Rachel Perkins	Ann Mariah Burton
Karen Perkins	Zoe Nikolos
Kaya Scheman	Olivia Palamaris

Kyle Sharp

Mike Kim

Stephanie Kontos

Sophie Behdani

Mary Grace Parker

Angelika Ballas

Courtney Sherbal

Lucy McLeod

Isabelle McMullen

Ellis Ewert

Michaela Kortaba

Adrielle Lee

Allison Parkhill

Caroline Kuhn

Erica Kontos

Sophia Roth

Landon Shelley

Jacqueline Contento

Julia Henegar

Grace Malakelis

Neha Kukreja

Lizzy Davidson

Clare Downey

Camille Monceaux

Riley Blair

Kit McNiff

Julia Weidman

Sara Tavakolian

Sara Evall

Isabella Reynolds

Andrew Elcock

Valerie Athanailos

Logan Welborn

Trinette Atri

Rachel Huang

Casey Chanler

Caroline Smith

Vasiliki Argeroplos

Valerie Athanailos

Lee Smallwood

Gabrielle Athanasia

Audrey Magnuson

Amelia Hunt

Helen Moffat

Renee Weisz

Abbie Gatewood

Meredith Vaughn

Anna Alexia Markouizos

Mary Kate Viceconte

Helen McGinnis

Bre Welles

Irena Pantazis

PART ONE

BRAINS, BEAUTY, BOSS: A LIFESTYLE

CHAPTER 1

THE INSPIRATION BEHIND IT ALL

———

"There is no perfect fit when you're looking for the next big thing to do. You have to take opportunities and make an opportunity fit for you, rather than the other way around. The ability to learn is the most important quality a leader can have."

—SHERYL SANDBERG[1]

In 1975, Meryl Streep was rejected from acting in the renowned film *King Kong* after being rudely scoffed at by director Dino De Laurentiis. Today, Streep holds the record number of Academy Award nominations out of any actor in the entire world.[2]

Tina Fey, the comedy queen of American television, began her career as a receptionist. She was nearly thirty years old

---

1   Jeff Haden, "17 Great Sheryl Sandberg Quotes on Success, Leadership, and Perseverance," *Inc.com*, March 30, 2018.
2   Harriet Alexander, "Meryl Streep told she was 'too ugly' to act in King Kong," *The Telegraph*, November 11, 2015.

when she became the first female head writer for *Saturday Night Live.*[3]

When young Anna Wintour worked for *Harper's Bazaar,* she was fired after nine months. For the past thirty years, she has been the editor-in-chief of *Vogue US*, one of the most iconic fashion magazines of the world.[4]

Let's also take a second to talk about Lizzo, the singer of the chart-topping hit "Truth Hurts." Lizzo lived out of her car for an entire year while trying to break into the music industry. Now, she is a three-time Grammy winner and an international figure for female empowerment.[5]

These stories not only highlight resilience, hard work, and passion, but they also display something society tends to overlook: the power of unconventionality.

From the start of our education, we are taught to follow conventional pathways to reach success. In kindergarten, we are taught we must color within the lines. In middle school, we are taught how to structure our essays with an introduction, three body paragraphs, and a conclusion—but don't worry, you can go *wild* with your one-line hook statement. In high school, we take standardized tests that rank us against each other on our ability to answer generic reading comprehension passages and questions on basic trigonometry. These

---

3   "41 Rocking Facts About Tina Fey," Factinate, accessed July 25, 2020.
4   "15 Women Who Became Successful Later in Life and Proved It's Never Too Late," Bright Side, accessed July 25, 2020.
5   Ibid.

standardized tests help determine our fate in the college admissions process.

Unfortunately, this trend also continues at the undergraduate level. In "Elite Universities Don't Get Failure," Joshua Spodek highlights how our education system values intellectual growth at all costs, compromising our ability to focus on connecting emotionally and socially with others. Instead of learning important skills for the workplace, we are taught to follow schedules, focus on facts, and choose our learning path from a list of subject areas. According to Spodek, "the behavior we teach is *compliance,* the opposite of thinking and acting for yourself."[6]

Given these circumstances, it is no wonder Gen Z strives to follow similar pathways to reach their career goals. Conventionality and following the status quo are ingrained within our minds from day one. Whether we realize it or not, the conventionality we are accustomed to can be very destructive for our careers, particularly among women.

According to a Hewlett Packard report, men will typically apply for a job if they meet 60 percent of the qualifications, while women will usually only apply to the same job if they meet 100 percent of the qualifications, implying women are less confident in the job application process than men.[7] Some researchers have expressed if women were more confident, they would apply to jobs at the same rate as their male

---

6 Joshua Spodek, "Elite Universities Don't Get Failure," *Inc.Com,* June 30, 2017.

7 Jack Zenger, "The Confidence Gap in Men and Women: Why It Matters and How to Overcome It," *Forbes,* April 8, 2018.

counterparts and ultimately enter job pipelines at similar rates.

When *Harvard Business Review* journalist, Tara Mohr, dug deeper to understand the intrinsic meaning behind this statistic, she found the issue was not confidence. In a survey of over one thousand men and women, predominately American professionals, she found that most women would not apply to roles because they did not meet all of the specific requirements on the checklist, *not* because they weren't confident. According to Mohr, "They didn't see the hiring process as one where advocacy, relationships, or a creative approach to framing one's expertise could overcome not having the skills and experience outlined in the job qualifications."[8]

Having the need to check off every item on a list of qualifications is solely one example of how conventionality can be detrimental for a woman's career trajectory. So many of our everyday choices and actions are inherently influenced by the institutional structures we have grown up with. From being taught to color within the lines to holding the misconception we must have a certain grade point average or academic background to win over an interviewer, conventionality inevitably impacts so many life decisions.

How do we change this? How can we reverse the conventionality we have known our entire lives? How can we become the leaders we aspire to be? Is there a true pathway to success?

---

8   Tara Mohr, "Why Women Don't Apply for Jobs Unless They're 100% Qualified," *Harvard Business Review*, August 25, 2014.

Success is not formulaic. It is not the same for everyone, and no two people have the same expectations or pathway to success. Conforming to the same notions we have been accustomed to our entire lives will not help us become extraordinary thinkers, just people who follow the rules extremely well.

* * *

Instead of trying to map out our futures, we must learn lessons from people who have served as mentors, people who have overcome obstacles, people who have completely shattered the status quo, and people who did so in a way that made lasting impacts in their respective industries.

Ironically enough, I initially experienced this realization in my junior year of high school on a bright pink futon. On a Sunday afternoon, I cracked open an ice-cold Diet Coke and began my pre-homework ritual of the week: I made myself comfortable on the futon, gathered my pens and highlighters, and opened up my laptop to read the latest news on Cosmopolitan.com. As I scrolled through celebrity gossip, lifestyle tips, and beauty advice, I came across an article called "Get That Life: How I Became the CEO of SoulCycle."[9]

Standing powerfully in her office space was Melanie Whelan, the CEO of SoulCycle. Her story was about resilience, hard work, and difficult career choices that ultimately led to her

---

9   Elizabeth Narins, "Get That Life: How I Became the CEO of SoulCycle," *Cosmopolitan.com*, December 26, 2016.

becoming the CEO of a high growth fitness company and brand.[10] As a woman seeking to enter the business world, I was immediately intrigued. Melanie never had a list to check off, nor a specific pathway she anticipated. She followed her intuition and worked extremely hard.

Melanie's story led me to an entire subsection of Cosmopolitan.com called "Get That Life" with dozens of short articles about amazing women sharing their secrets to success with all of the *Cosmo* readers.[11] I was introduced to powerful stories behind famous astrophysicists, celebrity manicurists, top executives, and even the story behind the editor of Cosmopolitan.com itself, Amy Odell. Each story I read was equally fascinating and inspiring. Soon after this discovery, my Sunday pre-homework routine became a little bit different. Instead of looking for the newest celebrity gossip or filling out quizzes on topics like which Kardashian child I identified with the most, I looked for the newest article in the "Get That Life" series.

As a sixteen-year-old girl whose last Google search was "How to Avoid Failing Your Driver's License Test Again," (it happened three times, oops), the "Get That Life" stories were truly inspirational. These stories were not just appealing to me because of their easy-to-read style and comical nature—they were so much more. These stories talked about women breaking into roles that had never been occupied by women before, real struggles among women in the workplace, and important lessons on resilience and self-discovery.

---

10   Ibid.
11   "Get That Life," *Cosmopolitan.com*, accessed July 25, 2020.

Fast forward two years: I was walking around the club fair at Duke University as an overly eager first-year student. I was immediately interested in Duke Association for Business Oriented Women, an organization promoting the intersection between female empowerment and the professional world.

Through each new speaker, workshop, and forum, I had access to new, exciting ideas about inclusion in the workplace, pathways to success, and what it truly meant to be a "go-getter" in modern times. After hearing certain speakers, I could even see some of them as young sixteen-year-olds who were once in my shoes, sitting on their futon couches surrounded by gum wrappers with no idea how their careers would ultimately pan out.

Soon enough, the key takeaways from the stories I read and events I attended began to connect together in surprising ways. Hearing and reading the success stories behind powerful women in business taught me more about discovering my own pathway and excelling as an entrepreneurial woman than any class had taught me. The stories entailed unconventionality, creative thinking, and challenging the status quo, notions I would have never followed in middle school while writing my perfect five-paragraph essays.

The same way narratives of success continue to shape my ideas and choices, I want these narratives to also shape the lives of women all across the world. From young Gen Z women eager to launch their own clothing start-ups to middle-aged women wanting to shift from mechanical engineer, to social media star, to everyone in between, inspirational firsthand accounts can be instrumental in peoples' lives.

These accounts can help you learn how to overcome obstacles, how to build confidence, and when to put your foot down if you think something is wrong.

Brains, Beauty, Boss is dedicated to sharing the powerful stories of women who have inspired me and are continuing to pave the way for women in their respective industries. I believe each and every woman has the **brains** to make an impact, their own authentic **beauty**, and the **boss** mentality to chase after their dreams like no other. In my book, I had the opportunity to dive deep into the pathways of *Forbes* 30 Under 30 women to capture their mentalities, their approaches to success, and the struggles they faced in reaching their goals.[12]

Each year, *Forbes* receives thousands of nominations, which are then narrowed down and sent to a group of judges for each specific industry. Anyone has the opportunity to be nominated for one of *Forbes* 30 Under 30 awards, and I had the chance to hear from self-made stars who truly stood out to me.

Through interviewing powerful women on the *Forbes* 30 Under 30 list, I heard the fascinating stories of women making FAFSA forms accessible to the most underprivileged populations of the world, women who are developing innovative clean energy solutions, women who have become international media icons, and many, many more. I have even spoken with the former editor of Cosmopolitan.com, the same

---

12   "Meet the Top Young Entrepreneurs of the Forbes Under 30 2020 List," *Forbes*, accessed July 3, 2020.

website that inspired me to write this book. Each individual story not only provides insight toward the principles of success, but also emphasizes there is no formulaic path or system for young women to reach their goals.

While examining different pathways to success, these stories also outline how different women have overcome obstacles in the workplace, from the many facets of Impostor Syndrome, to systematic flaws present in many industries. Each chapter highlights the mindset the *Forbes* women have used to build confidence, achieve their goals, and reign over Impostor Syndrome. In a society where so many people think they must follow very particular steps to become successful, *Brains, Beauty, Boss* displays how success stems from an individual mindset. Through writing this book, I realized *Brains, Beauty, Boss* is a mindset anyone and everyone can achieve—we just have to unlock our potential.

My goal is to empower all women so that we can reach our goals while becoming the leaders and creators we aspire to be. This book is for women interested in areas ranging from science, to history, to social entrepreneurship, to social media, to health care, and it is for entrepreneurs, scientists, teachers, corporate executives, and everyone in between. Kim Kardashian, if you're reading this, it's even for you.

CHAPTER 2

IMPOSTOR ALERT!

———

Imagine you are watching the season premiere of *The Bachelorette*, season fifteen.[13] Hannah Brown is standing powerfully, waiting for a group of thirty men who are smiling on the outside, but on the inside are gladiators ready to battle for her sweet, Alabama heart. It's time for first impressions. Jonathan comes in with a full pizza, Connor S. jumps over a fence to greet her, Ryan comes in on roller skates, and Joe jumps out of a box.[14] It is literally simp nation. As soon as the introductions are done, Hannah stands before all thirty of the men who are lined up in perfect rows. This is one of the most iconic moments of the entire season. Once you have this image in mind, add one more bachelorette. Let's say, Hannah Brown's best friend who is now on the show to add some typical reality TV **drama**. Two women, thirty men, and the host Chris Harrison, of course. As of May 2019,

———

13 *The Bachelorette*, season 15 episode 1, "Week 1: Season Premiere," directed by Ken Fuchs, aired May 13, 2019, on ABC.

14 Ibid.

this female-to-male ratio is the same ratio of female-to-male CEOs at *Fortune* 500 companies.[15]

Fortune magazine publishes the *Fortune* 500 list each year to rank five hundred of the largest US corporations by their sales revenue from the previous fiscal year.[16] Making it onto this list is a huge achievement most CEOs dream of, and this list marks the epitome of success for many businesses. Out of the five hundred companies featured on the *Fortune* 500 list in 2019, thirty-three of these companies had female CEOs: only 6.6 percent of the entire group. The most startling aspect of this statistic is that a *Fortune* 500 list with 6.6 percent of the CEOs being female is considered groundbreaking, as this is one of the highest percentages of female CEOs the list has ever seen before.

Why is this the case? Dozens of research reports and studies have thoroughly examined the issue of gender inequality in the workplace, and it is clear society is in a slow, uphill battle toward reaching complete gender equality.

MAINTAINING FAMILY DUTIES CAN POSE A MAJOR OBSTACLE FOR WOMEN IN BUSINESS:

One of the major issues women face in career advancement is maintaining work-life balance. Women typically perform more family duties than men, and these family duties can be major impediments in their careers. According to Indra

---

15   Claire Zillman, "The Fortune 500 Has More Female CEOs Than Ever Before," *Fortune*, May 16, 2019.

16   Fred Decker, "What Are the Qualifications to Be Listed as a Fortune 500 Company?" *Bizfluent*, October 22, 2018.

Nooyi, former CEO of Pepsi, "as you get to middle management, women rise to those positions, and then that's the childbearing years. And when they have children, you know, it's difficult to balance having children, your career, your marriage, and you know, be a high potential out-performer who's going to grow in the company and an organization that's—you know, every one of them is a pyramid, so it starts to thin out as you move up."[17]

Indra Nooyi was one of the only female CEOs of a *Fortune* 500 company prior to leaving Pepsi in 2018, and she emphasizes the mid-career gap between males and females very well.[18] When women leave their jobs for maternity leave or to take care of their children, it inevitably gives their male counterparts an advantage. This ultimately leads to greater promotion opportunities for men and less opportunities for women to reach upper management roles.

GENDER BIAS IN THE WORKPLACE—WHAT WE SEE AND WHAT WE DON'T SEE:

In a different light, gender bias is also a major contributing factor to gender inequalities in the workplace. Sheryl Sandberg, chief operating officer of Facebook, thoroughly examines this issue in her best-seller *Lean In*. According to Sandberg, "We expect men to be assertive, look out for themselves, and lobby for more—so there's little downside when they do it. But women must be communal and

---

17   Ari Shapiro, "Why Major U.S. Companies Still Have So Few Women CEOs," August 10, 2018, in All Things Considered, hosted by Ari Shapiro, podcast.

18   Ibid.

collaborative, nurturing and giving, focused on the team and not themselves, lest they be viewed as self-absorbed. So, when a woman advocates for herself, people often see her unfavorably."[19]

Sandberg directly examines how perceptions of how men and women should act in the workplace end up working against women.[20] It is very difficult for many women to find the perfect in between: not too aggressive, but not too easygoing. But, when women gain the confidence to assert themselves, reaching into the "aggressive" side can create a negative impression.

I will never forget the first time I was called bossy. It was in third grade science class and we had to try and build a bridge that could hold the most weight. If we won, we had the chance to pick three pieces of candy from the infamous treasure chest. Seems easy, right? Trust me, it was not.

We only had three materials: string, cardboard, and straws. When my group started working, they wanted to do the bare minimum and then go to lunch (I honestly don't blame them, there were definitely SpongeBob popsicles in the cafeteria that day). Instead, I told the group we had to make two different designs, talk about the pros and cons of each, and then build the bridge as perfectly as we could. Suddenly, one of the twerps named Jack said, "You're being so bossy. You need

---

19   Rachel Gillett and Madison Hoff, "Gender Bias Could Make It Harder for Women to Become CEO, According to a Recent Study," *Business Insider*, April 17, 2020.

20   Sheryl Sandberg, *Lean In: Women, Work and the Will to Lead*, (New York: Alfred A. Knopf, 2013).

to chill out." As my blood raced, I couldn't believe what I had just heard. Me? Bossy? All I was trying to do was make sure the group did well, and *this* was how I was rewarded? Absolutely not!

In this moment, I figured it out. People call leaders bossy, and people throw the word around when they see a young woman who is assertive with what she wants. Jack—if you're reading this, you still owe me an apology.

* * *

Rachel Thomas, one of the founders of the "Ban Bossy" campaign, reveals how the stigma against assertive women begins at childhood and continues throughout their professional careers. According to Thomas, "if you assert yourself, you're less well-liked," and "if you don't assert yourself enough, you're not seen as competent."[21] This perpetuates a disastrous cycle because if women do not assert themselves and advocate for themselves, who will?

Thomas' insight is also supported by a Lean In/McKinsey & Company survey from 2016. This survey found that women who negotiated for promotions had a 30 percent higher chance of being labeled as "bossy" or "aggressive," rather than confident or empowered.[22]

---

21 Drake Baer, "Here's Why Banning the Word 'Bossy' Is Great for Women," *Business Insider*, March 24, 2014.

22 Susan Chira, "Why Women Aren't C.E.O.S, According to Women Who Almost Were," *New York Times*, July 21, 2017.

Ultimately, many female leaders are stuck in situations where standing up for themselves can work against them, while saying nothing can also work against them. From birth, young men are usually taught to be aggressive, while many young women are taught to be elegant and poised. So, when women act more like stereotypical male figures, it can appear very unusual, and is oftentimes unfavorable amongst male coworkers and society. One example of this took place during the recent scandals with Facebook. During the scandals, COO Sheryl Sandberg was portrayed to the media as a villain, whereas CEO Mark Zuckerberg came across as a "flawed, yet forgivable tech whiz."[23] The media's response in this particular situation is solely one example of how women and men in leadership positions can be portrayed to society in vastly different ways for making the same mistakes.[24]

In addition, "in-group favoritism" is vastly present in the workplace. According to an article from *The Conversation*, "people tend to evaluate others who are similar to them more favorably. This bias works against women because nearly 80 percent of board members in large US public companies are men. These are the people responsible for hiring and paying CEOs, after all."[25]

This means that in-group favoritism directly leads to less women brought into upper level management pipelines.

---

23 Kirsty Trafford-Owens, "Women Are 'Bossy,' Men Are 'Leaders': How Women in Power Are Perceived Differently to Men," *Druthers Search*, January 19, 2019.

24 Ibid.

25 Michael Holmes, "Why Are There So Few Women CEOs?" *The Conversation*.

Without a strong system for women to enter the CEO role, they are inevitably excluded from this position.

WE ARE SURROUNDED BY IMPOSTORS:

Lastly, there is a phenomenon so grand in the workplace it has its own name: Impostor Syndrome. *TIME* magazine refers to Impostor Syndrome as the "idea that you've only succeeded due to luck, and not because of your talent and qualifications."[26] Impostor Syndrome can exist amongst women who have just received their dream promotions, women who make the *Forbes* 30 Under 30 list, and even women who are running for office.

The truth is that a horrifically high number of women suffer from Impostor Syndrome, and it continues to inhibit them from reaching their highest potential. According to research from NatWest, "60 percent of women who have considered starting a business did not because of a lack of confidence, not feeling like the type of person who could start a business or feeling they did not deserve to succeed despite their skills."[27] Impostor Syndrome is known as "women's silent career killer."[28]

Impostor Syndrome is not called the "silent career killer" because it is impossible to overcome. The main reason Impostor Syndrome is so terrifying is because so many women

---

26 Abigail Abrams, "Yes, Impostor Syndrome Is Real. Here's How to Deal with It," *Time*, June 20, 2018.

27 Rebecca Burn-Callander, "Imposter syndrome: women's silent career killer," *The Telegraph*, May 16, 2019.

28 Ibid.

experience it without even knowing. Women suffering from Impostor Syndrome can be anywhere: from your local cafe, to your Monday morning meeting, to your hair salon, to your library, to everywhere in between.

Nearly 70 percent of people experience Impostor Syndrome.[29] It is a very real phenomenon that inevitably contributes to lack of confidence, lack of trust, and lack of career advancement in the workplace.

In Dr. Valerie Young's book *The Secret Thoughts of Successful Women: Why Capable People Suffer from the Impostor Syndrome and How to Thrive in Spite of It,* she examines how people suffer from Impostor Syndrome through different frameworks of competence types. You can determine your competence type(s) through asking yourself the following question:

What would it take for me to be competent at _____?

According to Dr. Young, "Every impostor on the planet has a distorted view of competence. However, not all impostors skew it the same way."[30] To convey the different ways people suffering from Impostor Syndrome falsely perceive what it takes to be competent, Dr. Young generated five different competence types: "The Perfectionist, The Superwoman/man,

---

29 Danielle Page, "How Impostor Syndrome Is Holding You Back at Work," *Better by Today*, October 25, 2017.

30 Valerie Young, *The Secret Thoughts of Successful Women: Why Capable People Suffer from the Impostor Syndrome and How to Thrive in Spite of It,* (New York: Crown Business, 2011).

The Natural Genius, The Soloist, and The Expert."[31] Prior to reading Dr. Young's book, I did not even realize I was personally suffering from Impostor Syndrome until I read the description for the competence type of "The Perfectionist."[32] Then, I realized, *Oh. My. God. That's me.*

To better communicate the different ways that impostors skew the idea of competence, I developed five case studies that encompass the five competence types Dr. Young highlighted in her book—with a modern-day twist. These case studies are unique individuals who embody realistic experiences of women today. You may find that you relate to one of these women, a few of these women, or even all of them.

TYPE A: SARAH, "THE PERFECTIONIST":[33]

Every morning, Sarah goes to Starbucks and orders the same iced matcha latte before dropping her three kids Piper, Cade, and Jessica off at school. She makes the same lunch for them each day: peanut butter and jelly, fresh apples, a bag of pretzels, and a handwritten note. After reading the latest *Morning Brew* article, she heads to her job as a digital media consultant for a global marketing firm.

When she enters the office, she is given a new task. By the end of the week, she has to develop a unique media strategy for a chic bathing suit line to reach new customers. The swimwear company's goal is to increase revenue by 5 percent within

---

31   Ibid.
32   Ibid.
33   Ibid.

the next month. Immediately, she outlines a detailed plan and delegates tasks to her analysts. Every hour, she checks in on the analysts to ensure they are following her directions. In the meantime, she works on every component of the marketing plan, focusing on little details for hours at a time. One night, she even stays at work for five extra hours to perfect her pitch.

Once Sarah's team submits the final pitch to the bathing suit company, they receive rave reviews. The CEO of the swimwear company calls Sarah personally and thanks her for her efforts, as their sales increased by 7 percent, 2 percent more than their original goal.

Despite the praise Sarah receives, she continues to contemplate:

"A 7 percent increase in revenue is great, but what could have led to a 10 percent increase in revenue?"

"OMG. Why was the third slide in the presentation deck teal when I asked for it to be turquoise?"

"What would have happened if I had delegated the tasks a little bit more quickly to my analysts?"

Sarah's mindset in this situation is in direct alignment with "The Perfectionist."[34]

---

34   Ibid.

"The Perfectionist" is the person who is obsessed with everything falling into perfect alignment with their highly ambitious goals. They are the type of people who score 99 percent on their math tests, but are upset why they missed the one point. They are also the type of people who chase after excellence and go to extreme measures to achieve it. This type of attitude can be present in the workplace, at home, at the local bank, or even in the grocery store.[35]

If you have ever thought to yourself, "Why did I deserve this?" or "I will not be happy unless this is done perfectly," or "I need to make sure everyone follows my directions exactly," you more than likely relate to "The Perfectionist." Women who connect to "The Perfectionist" accomplish great feats but feel inadequate despite their hard work and effort.

TYPE B: BLAIR, "THE NATURAL GENIUS":[36]

Blair is the owner and head chef of B's Sweet Southern Cafe. As Blair grew up, she fell in love with Southern cooking. After finishing her homework each night, she helped her grandmother cook the family dinner. From sweet potato casserole, to pumpkin pie, to hand-breaded fried chicken, to the most savory cheddar biscuits, Blair learned how to perfect it all.

Upon graduating high school, Blair went to culinary school. After saving up money and working as a part-time chef at three different restaurants, Blair earned enough money to pursue her dream of opening her own restaurant.

---

35 Ibid.
36 Ibid.

Located in the heart of Manhattan, B's Sweet Southern Cafe is a fascinating contrast to the modern, trendy restaurants New York City is known for. From businesspeople wanting a home-cooked meal for their lunch break, to young, aspiring artists, to high schoolers who just finished their final exams, B's Sweet Southern Cafe is the perfect place to unwind and relax over delicious grits and sweet tea. Blair's walls are lined with awards for her famous cornbread, fried chicken, and delicious Southern dishes, and she is well-known throughout all of the East Coast for her unique culinary techniques.

On the three-year anniversary of Blair's business launch, she receives a life-changing offer. On one Sunday afternoon, one of the casting producers from Gordon Ramsay's famous show, *Hell's Kitchen,* comes to B's Sweet Southern Cafe for chicken and waffles. After tasting what he calls the "best Southern food of his life," he gives Blair an offer to come on the show. *Hell's Kitchen* is a competitive gameshow where the nation's top chefs battle head-to-head against each other, and the winner receives $250,000 and the opportunity to be an executive chef at one of Ramsay's renowned restaurants.

At first, Blair is ecstatic. She has never had an opportunity like this before, and she knows B's Sweet Southern Cafe would explode with publicity if she went on the show. She could expand her franchise, pay off her culinary school debt, and move into a bigger apartment. But she begins to doubt her abilities.

Immediately, Blair thinks to herself, "I specialize in Southern cooking, and on *Hell's Kitchen,* the chefs face challenges where they have to showcase their skills across all different types of cuisine. Southern cooking comes easily to me because I have had so much experience in it, but other types of cuisine are way harder for me to grasp. Should people even view me as a professional chef?" Initially, Blair tells the casting producer no. She feels comfortable where she is, and does not think she is worthy enough to be on the show.

Soon after, Blair calls her sister to discuss what just happened. Immediately, Blair's sister outlines all of the reasons why Blair would make a perfect contestant for *Hell's Kitchen*. She talks about how Blair has always been persistent and hardworking, and that she just has to put in more effort to learn new cuisine types outside of Southern cooking.

Once Blair gets off of the phone with her sister, she calls the producer back, and gets a spot on the next season of *Hell's Kitchen*. In the second week of shooting, Blair wins her first competition. She advances all the way to the final round, and ends up winning the entire competition with her own unique take on a pasta primavera dish, an Italian specialty.

In this situation, Blair connects to the "The Natural Genius" competence type.[37] "The Natural Genius" measures competence in terms of ease and speed.[38] They think to themselves, "if I was truly competent at my job, this task wouldn't be this hard." In Blair's case, the task is learning types of cuisine outside of Southern cooking.

---

37 Ibid.

38 Ibid.

According to Dr. Young, "The Natural Genius," "[expects] to know without being taught…excel without effort, and to get it right on the first attempt."[39] In Blair's situation, she does not want to go on *Hell's Kitchen* initially because she thinks it would be too difficult for her to learn new culinary techniques as a Southern cooking specialist. Ironically, she ends up winning the competition for a dish that wasn't even Southern.

The "Natural Genius" can be the first-year student entering an elite university for the first time, a debate champion heading to nationals, or even a fashion designer who has to transform a new line for some of the world's toughest critics.

TYPE C: RACHEL, "THE SUPERWOMAN":[40]

Rachel is twenty years old and is a third-year student in college. She studies Economics and Finance, and she just landed her dream internship, working part time at a local investment bank during the fall semester outside of class. She went through hours of networking, cold calls, informational events, and coffee chats to make it this far. On the first day of work, she struts into the office with her new Aritzia dress and her classic Gucci sleds. She wants to appear confident, yet eager to learn. Outgoing, yet poised.

On top of the part-time internship, Rachel is president of her university's student body, she is an active member of her

---

39 Ibid.
40 Ibid.

sorority, she runs an organization for women in business, and she plays on the club field hockey team. At the end of Rachel's first day, she sees five missed calls from one of her friends on the club field hockey team.

Immediately, Rachel realizes that she forgot about her club field hockey game that night. She sprints to her car, changes into her uniform, and makes her way to the game facility located thirty minutes away.

During the car ride to the game, Rachel thinks to herself, "I should not have forgotten about the game…I know I have a lot on my plate, but there is no reason why I shouldn't have been able to do it all."

Many young people like Rachel can connect to "The Super-woman." "The Superwoman" expects to do it all. Even when they accomplish great feats, they believe that they can do more. Rather than reflecting on the fact that she committed to too many things, Rachel was extremely hard on herself for forgetting about the game.

According to Dr. Young, "The Superwoman" tells themself, "If I were really competent, I would be able to do it all."[41]

TYPE D: ALLEGRA, "THE SOLOIST":[42]

Allegra is a med-school graduate who is beginning her first year of residency. If you watch *Grey's Anatomy*, this program

---

41   Ibid.
42   Ibid.

is the Seattle Grace residency program of the Northwest: intense, cut-throat, and inevitably dramatic.

On the first day of the program, Allegra and the other residents are brought into a lab with simulators of human bodies. These simulators can breathe and bleed, and have very similar features to actual human structures. The head of training tells them their first task is to insert an IV into the simulator's arm, and if they cannot find a vein, they should ask for help.

Immediately, the residents analyze the veins of the simulators to determine where the IV's should be inserted. Allegra anxiously searches for the vein, but she cannot find it. Instead of asking for help, she continues to search. In her head, she thinks, "If I ask for help, it will show a sign of ineptness. If I am truly qualified to be in this program, I should be able to figure this out on my own."

After Allegra continues working for ten minutes, the head of training insists she should help Allegra so she is not behind for the next exercise. After seeing where the head of training places the IV, Allegra realizes that this was not a situation she could have resolved on her own; she needed help from the start.

Allegra directly connects to the competence type of "The Soloist."[43]

_____

43   Ibid.

"The Soloist" views competence as "solo, unaided achievement."[44] They worry that they are inadequate if they have to seek out help, and only truly value accomplishments that they reached entirely on their own.[45] The mentality of "The Soloist" can be common amongst the entrepreneurial community. Some entrepreneurs obsess over the idea of jumpstarting ideas on their own, and do not reach out for help when it is necessary. This leads to the development of unrealistic expectations and unnecessary stress.

TYPE E: HANNA, "THE EXPERT":[46]

Hanna is a forty-five-year-old woman who researches solutions for clean water in areas of the world where access to clean, safe water is a pressing issue. For three years she lived in Ghana, working directly with local leaders and different NGO's to develop innovative solutions for access to clean water.

After working in Ghana, she spent eight years spearheading a new initiative for a nonprofit addressing the global water crisis. This past year, one of her colleagues sent her the application for a grant to develop new, cutting-edge technology to develop further solutions for access to clean water.

When Hanna read the application, she was immediately intimidated. To apply for this grant, the applicant required "in-depth knowledge of potential clean water solutions"

---

44 Ibid.
45 Ibid.
46 Ibid.

and "extensive experience in developing solutions for clean water." Although Hanna spent the majority of her post-graduate career working directly in the areas the description entailed, she did not think she was qualified to apply.

After hearing Hanna was not going to apply for the grant, her personal mentor wanted to discuss her concerns. Hanna said she was very interested in the opportunity, but did not think she had enough knowledge about clean water access to be a strong candidate for the grant. After Hanna's mentor outlined all of the reasons why she would make a phenomenal candidate, she hesitantly decided to apply. Three months later, Hanna received the notification that she was awarded the grant.

Hanna falls in direct alignment with the mentality of "The Expert" in this situation. Even when "The Expert" has evidence of their knowledge or experience in an area, they still worry that they do not know enough.[47] The fear that they'll never know enough keeps them from applying to jobs, going for promotions, or starting businesses unless they can go in with the unrealistic expectation that they know 150 percent. Even when women like Hanna truly do have unquestionable expertise, people who identify with this competence type rarely feel deserving of the title, "Expert."[48]

---

47   Ibid.
48   Ibid.

HOW SARAH, BLAIR, RACHEL, ALLEGRA, AND HANNA PLAY INTO THE BIG PICTURE:

Although the stories of Sarah, Blair, Rachel, Allegra, and Hanna are each very different from one another, they all exemplify different feelings tied to Impostor Syndrome. Impostor Syndrome can lead individuals to believe they did not deserve their achievements or status, or that they accomplished great things due to luck.

In a society where Impostor Syndrome is incredibly common, it is important for us to find solutions to help individuals break free from this pressing issue. The first step is helping others acknowledge if they connect to any of the competence types of Impostor Syndrome. The next step is to hear stories of women who faced the same feelings and discovered ways to break free.

In my journey writing this book, I have heard stories from women on the *Forbes* 30 Under 30 list challenging gender stereotypes, breaking into new industries, overcoming great obstacles, and overcoming Impostor Syndrome.

They are incredible accounts of resilience, perseverance, and hard work. My interviews with these women highlight the power of unconventionality, and how lacking answers about the future can sometimes be the most beneficial tool for young people beginning their careers.

With their advice, all young people entering the workforce can come one step closer to reaching their personal version of success.

PART TWO

THE ICONIC TRAILBLAZERS

CHAPTER 3

WOLF OF WALL STREET...WHO?

———

During my sophomore year at Duke, I distinctly remember a cold, December night in the library when I was studying for the technical portion of an investment banking interview. For weeks, I recited my résumé by heart, reviewed over vault guide questions, and closely followed the transactions of major companies I could be asked about. My desk was decorated with empty Diet Coke cans, colorful flashcards about discounted cash flow analysis, in addition to Extra gum wrappers. I used to swear by the mint flavor, thinking it infinitely increased my productivity. Spoiler alert—it did not.

The end goal? Landing an internship on Wall Street, one of the most sought-after opportunities for college students interested in business. But, for students not pursuing careers in the financial services industry, what did Wall Street mean to them?

Soon after I experienced these thoughts, I asked some of my peers, "When you think about Wall Street, what comes to mind?" Their answers were fascinating, sometimes comical, but overall, very eye-opening (for privacy reasons, the names of my friends were changed).

"Umm, probably a bunch of men yelling around a trading floor. Oh, and that movie with Leonardo DiCaprio, right?" says Sara with confidence.

"I see dollar signs everywhere," says Raquel.

"Umm, when I think about Wall Street, the first thing that comes to mind is a nervous intern running into a big building carrying four Starbucks lattes," says Robert as he laughs loudly. His experience was way too specific. It definitely hit close to home.

"I envision a ton of guys sitting around a table overlooking New York City wearing super high-end suits. They are probably talking about the score of last night's game or their vacation house in the Hamptons," says Niko.

Although I only asked four of my peers for their responses (two guys and two girls), their answers gave me a pretty good idea of how the financial services industry is envisioned by young people.

Immediately, I noticed all four of my peers recognized the financial services industry as a male dominated space with lots of money, and not one of them mentioned the presence of strong, powerful women. You don't have to work in finance to know it is a very male-dominated space. But, throughout history, women have been very transformative in this arena, shaping the industry in a very positive way.

THE QUEENS WHO PAVED THE WAY IN FINANCE:

In the early nineteenth century, Abigail Adams, the wife of President John Adams, became the first female investor. While John served in the war, Abigail managed the household finances.[49] John wanted Abigail to invest their excess cash in farmland, but instead, Abigail invested this money in government bonds.[50] Was her investment worth it? Absolutely. Abigail saw a return of more than 400 percent on her investments.[51] This means if she invested $100, she earned $400, and ended up with five times the amount she first started with. Abigail went on to use this money to support other women, strengthening the female empowerment movement of the time.[52] Although Abigail's husband was the president, she was a queen like no other.

In the 1870s, Victoria Woodhull and her younger sister, Tennessee "Tennie" Claflin, made history on Wall Street.[53] These two became the first women to open a stock brokerage firm.[54] Within six weeks, the incredible duo made $700,000, an amount which equates to thirteen million dollars in

---

49   Paige Harris, "Women's History Month: Women in Finance," *Primeway* (blog).

50   Ibid.

51   Ibid.

52   Ibid.

53   Susannah Broyles, "Revolutionary Sisters: Victoria Woodhull and Tennessee Claflin," *MCNY Blog: New York Stories* (blog), June 24, 2014.

54   Ibid.

modern times.[55] According to Victoria, "[I] went unto Wall Street, not particularly because I wanted to be a broker…but because I wanted to plant the flag of women's rebellion in the center of the continent."[56] Iconic.

Fast forward through history, and powerful woman Rosemary McFadden became the first female president of any stock or futures exchange in the US, while Muriel Faye Siebert became the first woman to purchase a seat on the New York Stock Exchange.[57] As headlines like "Now the Girls Want to Play" spread through Wall Street like wildfire, women began their slow, uphill battle in establishing themselves within the finance world.[58]

WOMEN IN THE FINANCIAL SERVICES INDUSTRY TODAY—WHAT'S CHANGED AND WHAT HASN'T:

In the financial services industry today, there has been tremendous progress in promoting greater inclusion of females. But there is still a lot of work that needs to be done. According to *Morningstar*, as of 2020, "women account for 22 percent of corporate boards, twice the figure in 2000."[59] Furthermore, according to the US Equal Employment Opportunity Commission, around 30 percent of senior officials and managers

---

55 Ibid.
56 Ibid.
57 Contentworks Agency, "Women Who Rocked the Finance World— Muriel Faye 'Mickie' Siebert," *Medium*, April 2, 2019.
58 Contentworks Agency, "Women Who Rocked the Finance World— Muriel Faye 'Mickie' Siebert," *Medium*, April 2, 2019.
59 Reshma Kapadia, "Women in Finance Are Rising—at Last," *Barron's*, March 6, 2020.

in finance and insurance industries are women.[60] These statistics are much better than they have been in the past, but if statistics like 22 percent and 30 percent are considered incredible accomplishments, there are a lot of systematic changes needed.

At large financial institutions, the conversation surrounding equal gender representation in the workplace is becoming more clear and transparent.

According to an Oliver Wyman report entitled "Women on Financial Services 2020," "Many executives in the industry have felt a shift in dialogue in recent years. It is no longer box-ticking; gender diversity is now recognized as a strategic issue that impacts business outcomes. We are seeing more creativity and commitment in attracting, recruiting, and retaining women, with senior leadership starting to be held to account by linking results to remuneration. Tactical initiatives are starting to make a real change."[61]

Firms are seeing that incorporating more women into management pipelines helps them perform better and ultimately make more money.

On the other hand, the Oliver Wyman report also highlights how work-life balance, bias surrounding promotions, and flexibility remain structural challenges in promoting gender diversity in the financial services industry.[62] The mid-ca-

---

60   Ibid.
61   "Women in Financial Services 2020," Oliver Wyman, 2020.
62   Ibid.

reer gap between men and women is widely evident due to maternity leave.[63] Furthermore, there can be unconscious bias in the promotion process while judging an individual's ability to serve as an effective leader.[64] The next step beyond recognizing these structural challenges is to tackle them head-on. While most of these firms explicitly state how important gender diversity is in promoting business outcomes, there are still major steps that need to be taken in its implementation.

SO, WHAT IS NEXT FOR WOMEN IN FINANCE?

As a woman who plans to enter the financial services industry, I have had the opportunity to work at two firms championing the empowerment of women while promoting the development of women as mentors, bosses, and strong leaders. In fact, nearly every weekend of my sophomore year at Duke, different firms flew me into New York City for diversity conferences. At these conferences, I heard from top executives, diversity recruiters, and young analysts (all of whom were women) about their positive experiences in the industry. Additionally, I met hundreds of other women in college also interested in the financial services industry.

When I heard personal accounts from the women at the firms, I became extremely excited about entering the financial services industry, and I realized something huge: building a sense of community with women can truly make a difference in how young people enter the job search process. Having

---

63 Ibid.
64 Ibid.

strong mentors and believing you are going to be included in a space can truly make a difference while applying for jobs, or even entering certain industries. I think that every single industry needs to implement pipeline programs similar to those in the financial services industry so that more women are inclined to apply for roles, and stay at firms.

When I began my first internship in the financial services industry, I spent a lot of my free time reading about powerful women in finance who had risen in the industry very early on. The story of Gina Kirch, the woman who became the youngest director of BlackRock globally, immediately caught my attention. I had the phenomenal opportunity to interview Gina, and I think her story is inspirational and empowering. It highlights how hard work and passion can truly bring you success.

WHAT THE BALLET WORLD AND CO-ED BASEBALL CAN TEACH YOU ABOUT MANAGING YOUR CAREER:

According to *Forbes*, Gina Kirch is a "Young Money Merchant" who is shaping financial markets.[65] She made history for being the youngest person to ever become a director at the world's largest asset management firm. She is a passionate advocate for female-led companies and underprivileged populations in the philanthropic sector, as well as those entering the venture capital world. On top of all of this, she is only thirty-one years old.

---

65   Oliver Smith, "30 Under 30 Europe: The Young Money Merchants Shaping Financial Markets In 2019," *Forbes*, February 12, 2019.

In 2018, Gina Kirch rightfully earned her spot on the *Forbes* 30 Under 30 list in the finance sector. According to Data USA, the average age of female financial managers is forty-five-and-a-half.[66] Gina reached this point when she was only twenty-eight years old, nearly seventeen years ahead of the average time frame. In my interview with Gina, she shared her secrets to success, and how she rose to the top so quickly in a heavily male-dominated industry.

Ironically enough, Gina's drive for success began at the same age she was probably running around the playground and watching Barney. When Gina was three years old, she tried out for the NYC Ballet and was cut because her neck wasn't long enough. This actually ended up being one of the most formative events in her life.

"Being cut from the NYC ballet served as a constant reminder to me that even if you work extremely hard, sometimes opportunities are simply not available to you due to factors outside your control," says Gina.

This "underdog" story made Gina realize that she wanted to focus on challenging the status quo and helping other underdogs, too. Gina became captain of the co-ed baseball team in her area, wanting to break into a sport women were not traditionally a part of. Gina was later admitted into Columbia University, where she became an English, history, and anthropology major. After internships in fashion, film, and philanthropy, she realized her strengths fit best in a role in the financial services industry.

---

66 "Financial Managers," Data USA, accessed June 25, 2020.

GINA'S PATHWAY TO SUCCESS—THE ART OF NETWORKING AND BUILDING CONNECTIONS:

When Gina entered BlackRock as an analyst in 2011, they had recently completed the acquisition of Barclays Global Investors.

"On the first day at my desk following analyst training, a number of us came to find our teams were still dismantled, managers made redundant, and while HR communicated to us we still had a position within the organization, we were not quite sure what it would be. In the midst of the chaos, I relied on the strong network I'd built up internally during my internships, accepted any projects which came my way, honed in on skills I felt would be able to set myself apart, and maintained a smile on my face," says Gina.

Gina opened herself up to many new opportunities, numerous outside her realm of comfort. She recounted how she even served as somewhat of an "internal consultant" within the firm at twenty-two years old. For five years, Gina worked in the US Defined Contribution Distribution Group, where she worked on market research, strategic planning, and solutions delivery with large insurance companies and corporations to ultimately help individuals retire with confidence. Gina describes this sector as being "not the sexiest area to work in," but definitely meaningful for individuals and her career early on. The US Defined Contribution Distribution Group formed a significant part of BlackRock's business, and as Gina became promoted from analyst to associate to vice president in this group, she gained even more notoriety within the firm.

After establishing herself as a powerful go-getter at Black-Rock, Gina was asked to move to London to join Strategic Partnerships & DC Investments. In less than two years, she was promoted to director, becoming the youngest director BlackRock ever had. While working in this role, she maintained her focus on supporting underdogs as a co-chair of BlackRock Gives, the firm's global philanthropic organization, as well as becoming an angel investor for companies focused on I&D, wellness, and education. Investments included companies like Headstart and InsideOut, which were transforming the diversity recruiting landscape and mental health dilemma for employees, respectively. Because 10 percent of BlackRock's revenue was driven in the UK and it was host to one of the largest employee bases for the firm globally, Gina had the opportunity to advocate for causes she was passionate about while working at a multi-trillion-dollar asset management firm.

Although Gina worked extremely hard and diligently, this was not the only reason she rose up in the industry so quickly. One of the biggest factors she attributes to her success is having both mentors and sponsors.

"A lot of people ask for mentors at work, which is great, but you need both mentors and sponsors to rise within any organization. Mentors are people with whom you create more informal relationships, who you can ask questions to and receive advice from. They help serve as advisors and build up your confidence. Sponsors are people who will advocate for your advancement in a company, making them significant contributors to your progression," says Gina.

Gina referenced Anne Ackerley, the head of BlackRock's Retirement Group, as one of her sponsors, along with Dominik Rohe, the head of Latin America for BlackRock. Having strong sponsors, both male and female, can truly make a difference in a hardworking woman's career trajectory. Through continual advice from different mentors and sponsors, Gina learned "the art of the ask."

Gina used "the art of the ask" to reference how people should ask for promotions, enhanced compensation, and how to generally advocate for themselves in the workplace.

"If you're doing well at a company, you should be rewarded; asking for more when you're deserving of it is truly important. I see a ton of women who deserve more in the workplace but are hesitant to voice their opinions," says Gina.

In addition, Gina stressed the importance of being nice and respectful. It is definitely important to be your own person and to stand your ground. But, if you are a terror to work with, you are bound to make many enemies very quickly.

Think about *The Office* and the workplace dynamic at Dunder Mifflin Inc. If Michael Scott had been a horrific boss, Pam, Jim, and even Dwight would have probably quit on day one.

After working at BlackRock full-time for eight years and becoming the company's youngest director in history, Gina decided to leave. Although she thoroughly enjoyed her experience at the firm and appreciated those who helped her along her journey, she saw an immense opportunity in an industry where she could combine her passion for helping underprivileged populations with her passion for investing: venture capital.

According to *Fortune* magazine, in venture capital specifically, the percentage of female decision makers as of 2020 is only 13 percent, and the percentage of venture capital dollars allocated to female founders is merely 2.8 percent.[67] These percentages were even lower when Gina entered into the venture capital world as a female founder and general partner.

"I decided to go into venture capital because I felt I could enhance the journeys of founders and thus the creation of positively impactful businesses," says Gina.

Following this mentality, Gina co-founded The Venture Collective, a venture capital firm focused on creating equal opportunities for all entrepreneurs, regardless of gender, race, and socioeconomic backdrop. The Venture Collective continues to invest in a diverse set of companies, from businesses creating the future of individualized pet health tech like DIG Labs, to companies helping special education students optimize their learning experience and outcomes like Lifted, to a company that has developed the world's first scalable platform to grow slaughter-free leather from stem cells called VitroLabs.[68]

---

67 Lizette Chapman and Bloomberg, "Venture capital, long a boy's club, makes some progress in adding women," *Fortune*, February 7, 2020.
68 "Our Past Investments," The Venture Collective, accessed June 25, 2020.

CULTIVATE YOUR SENSE OF SELF-WORTH—GINA'S ADVICE FOR YOUNG WOMEN:

Gina's pathway to date highlights hard work and resilience, but it also displays the importance of advocating for yourself. Throughout her time at BlackRock, she chased after new opportunities to advance her career, even moving to London in the process.

While speaking with Gina, I asked her what advice she would give young women entering their careers. She broke her tips down into four distinct points:

1. There is a big difference between confidence and arrogance. Walk into the room with confidence, and show the world your intelligence and authentic self.
2. Cultivate your sense of self-worth. You are amazing, and can do great things.
3. Oftentimes with jobs, men will apply if they meet two out of ten of the requirements, while women won't apply even if they meet eight out of ten of the requirements. Don't be afraid to take risks, even if you don't check every single box.
4. Use your voice to speak up. Instead of being reactive, be proactive. You should take initiative and ask for new opportunities.

Gina's story is not only relevant within the financial services industry, but it brings up many important points for women entering any job. Her four key takeaways highlight that success arises from being a strong leader and team player—not from just being book smart.

Gina's story also offers valuable lessons for women trying to break free from obstacles in the workplace like Impostor Syndrome. Think back to the story of Blair, "The Natural Genius."[69]

"The Natural Genius" tries to avoid new, uncertain situations, and they believe that "true competence means having inherent intelligence and ability."[70] Instead of avoiding new challenges, Gina has taken many risks throughout her journey, understanding there can be opportunities for great success.

Gina moved to Europe in her mid-twenties, she co-founded a venture capital firm, and she entered the financial services industry following one of the greatest economic crises of all time. While taking these risks, Gina cultivated her self-worth throughout the entire process. This helped her acknowledge she was fully capable of tackling any challenge she faced.

One way for "The Natural Genius" to overcome Impostor Syndrome is to follow Gina's approach of viewing risks through a different lens.[71] Instead of backing down from new opportunities that posed risks, Gina chased after them, and this mindset led her to where she is today. Through encouraging young women to be confident and proactive in chasing their goals, Gina is helping the next generation of professional women achieve success.

---

69 Valerie Young, *The Secret Thoughts of Successful Women: Why Capable People Suffer from the Impostor Syndrome and How to Thrive in Spite of It*, (New York: Crown Business, 2011).

70 Ibid.

71 Ibid.

Gina's advice has even led me to transform the way I think about my own career path, and how I act in the workplace. Instead of waiting for new opportunities to come naturally, I have become more proactive. Rather than listening to a presentation with a senior person where I think to myself, "Wow, that person is so accomplished, I wonder what it took for them to get to where they are." I will email them, remembering the "art of the ask." Even if I do not receive a reply or have the chance to speak with them, I exit my comfort zone, and create a platform for a potential new connection.

Although cultivating your self-worth can be a complex journey, it is crucial in the long run. Just like Gina mentioned in the interview, "You are powerful and important. Make sure you demonstrate it."

KEY TAKEAWAYS:

- The "art of the ask" is a game changer for women in the workplace. Advocating for yourself is incredibly important in ensuring you are being provided with the chance for promotions, enhanced compensation, and leadership opportunities.
- You need both mentors and sponsors in the workplace. Mentors are important for providing advice and guidance, but sponsors are crucial in advocating for your growth and development at a firm.
- You need to remind yourself you are amazing and worthy of accomplishing great things. Tell this to yourself every day—in front of the mirror, while brushing your teeth, in the car, wherever it is—do it at least once.

CHAPTER 4

GOING VIRAL

Would you rather read a news article about a peeping tom, or a woman battling for equality?

No, I'm serious, it's a genuine question...take a few seconds to think about it.

The answer should seem obvious, right? Surprisingly, the answer was not so obvious for the newsroom team at *Wichita Falls Record News* one morning.

One day, the female editors and journalists at *Wichita Falls Record News* switched roles with their male counterparts as part of a social experiment.[72] The men at *Wichita Falls Record News* were the ones traditionally in charge of deciding which stories would be featured due to their upper management roles.

---

72 Laurence Pantin, "When Women Run Newsrooms, Women Are in the News," *We News,* April 6, 2001.

While deciding which story to feature on the front page, the team had two choices: a story about a peeping tom (gross) and a story about women battling for equality.[73] The fact that an actual debate took place about which of these stories should be featured is comical on its own. Ultimately, the story about the woman fighting for equal rights won, but it was a long battle between the women and men to reach this decision.[74]

The women in charge won this argument due to the leadership positions they held for the day as part of the social experiment.[75] On any other day with the men in charge of front-page content, the story about the peeping tom would have won. Need I say it again—gross.

Although this story from one newsroom in Wichita Falls, Texas does not represent the entire scope of the media industry, it does highlight one major takeaway: when women have leadership roles in media, more women are featured positively in press, TV shows, radio, films—you name it.

According to Belinda Hopkinson, project consultant at UNESCO, "It's only when people are in decision-making positions—whether they are men or women, whatever cultural background, race, orientation they have—they have any influence on the programming or orientation of the media."[76] This means until women have more opportunities to rise in the media industry as top executives and leaders

---

73 Ibid.
74 Ibid.
75 Ibid.
76 Ibid.

who can make decisions about media content, the media content we see will inevitably be more focused on the interests of men.

EVOLUTION OF THE MEDIA INDUSTRY FOR WOMEN— WHERE THE GENDER GAP STILL PERSISTS:

Since the beginning of the media industry with Gutenberg's development of the printing press, the invention of the radio, and the start of broadcast television, the media industry has been overall dominated by men. Editors of the nation's most widely distributed newspapers are overwhelmingly white males.[77] Men earn substantially more than women in newsrooms at the *Associated Press, Los Angeles Times, The New York Times, San Francisco Chronicle, The Wall Street Journal*, and *The Washington Post*.[78] In addition, according to a study from USC's Annenberg Inclusion Initiative, women accounted for less than one-third of speaking characters in a huge number of films released from 2006 to 2017.[79]

Across various sectors of the media industry, men make more money than women, men have more speaking roles than women, and men have overall more control over what media we consume. The vast majority of platforms in the media industry are predominately controlled by men.[80]

---

77 "The Status of Women in U.S. Media 2019," Women's Media Center, accessed June 25, 2020.

78 Ibid.

79 Ibid.

80 Ibid.

Although there are sectors within the media industry that have made progress, this just means they are closer to reaching the fifty-fifty ratio between male and female leadership than in the past. Plenty of steps need to be taken before this ratio is actually reached, and women can be as equally represented as men in media leadership roles.

FEMALE VOICES CREATE FEMALE STARS:
Although there is a long way to go before women are represented just as equally as men in top media roles, it is clear that as women gain greater traction within this space, they are paving the way for greater inclusion in the industry as a whole.

Look at Shonda Rhimes, the executive producer of the award-winning series *Grey's Anatomy*.

On top of having a female protagonist as the main character, Rhimes creates female characters whose success stems from being unapologetically themselves. Spoiler alert: if you are still on season two, *please* skip the next paragraph.

From Dr. Miranda Bailey being promoted to the first female chief of the entire hospital, to Dr. Meredith Grey winning the prestigious Harper Avery award, to Dr. Izzie Stevens standing up against other doctors criticizing her for her past life as a lingerie model, Rhimes portrays women as resilient, confident, but most importantly, empowered. Instead of creating a primetime show solely focused on drama and romance, Rhimes uses her voice to bring light to important issues ranging from flaws in the healthcare system to domestic violence.[81]

From Tina Fey running the show at *Saturday Night Live*, to Mindy Kaling having her own series, to Oprah's world-famous talk show, women are crushing the game in the media world and it shows. TV shows and movies are no longer just highlighting the male "player" who talks to four girls at the same time, but also feature the girl dumping the guy holding her back in her career. Slowly but surely, the media industry is shifting from women being given the spotlight, to women creating the spotlight for themselves.

To hear about the paths of women who have created their own spotlight, I interviewed both Lizz Warner, the former director of video at BuzzFeed, and Sami Fishbein, the chief creative officer of the multimedia brand Betches. Both women landed a spot on the *Forbes* 30 Under 30 list through trailblazing in the media industry, and through maintaining their authentic, unique voices.

VIRAL TINDER DATES TO CROSS-COUNTRY CHEESE ROAD TRIPS—LIZZ WARNER'S RISE TO SUCCESS:

If you had to guess what a Tinder date from the Olympics, a coastal road trip centered around cheese, a video of a young girl eating a huge bowl of ramen, and a cupcake ATM all had in common, you would probably be super confused. Paradoxically enough, these were all viral videos produced by

---

81 *Grey's Anatomy,* season 12 episode 2, "Walking Tall," written by Shonda Rhimes, aired October 1, 2015, on ABC.

Lizz Warner, former director of video at BuzzFeed, fueling her rise to the top of the media industry.

I had the opportunity to interview Lizz and found out how her unique experiences came together to make her the powerful woman in media she is today. Lizz's authenticity and comical yet charismatic energy helped her stand out amongst thousands of other people in her field.

In the media industry, it is incredibly important for leaders to connect people and find places of common interest. Lizz Warner does this extremely well, and it helped her advance professionally at BuzzFeed, a company that connects people of all different ages and backgrounds.

FROM SUBURBIA TO LA:
Growing up, Lizz knew she wanted to enter the world of video production. In college, she majored in business and Spanish to diversify and augment her video production skills. During high school and college, she began working internships at television networks and in the news, which ultimately led to her working at MTV in New York.

One night, months before graduating, she was hanging out with her roommate and stumbled across a BuzzFeed video. Her roommate pointed out that the creative, comical tone established throughout BuzzFeed seemed to match Lizz's interest in video production along with her passion for creativity. Soon after, Lizz reached out to BuzzFeed and was able to set up an internship interview. After flying to California, she landed the gig. One week after graduation, she moved to LA and her career at BuzzFeed began.

"I loved working at BuzzFeed straight out of college. The company was young at the time, giving early hires creative freedom to experiment with new concepts. It fast-tracked us to learn all aspects of video production, unlike traditional television, where it takes a long time to prove you're good at one skill. I had the opportunity to make and learn from content delivered to millions of people immediately," says Lizz.

As she climbed the ladder at BuzzFeed, her content began to go super viral, leading to massive growth for the company. Through directing and producing videos like "Grandmas Skydive for the First Time," Lizz showcased her ability to find unique ways to grab viewers' attention.[82]

In less than two years, Lizz was promoted to supervising video producer, where she managed and advised producers in both LA and many of the international BuzzFeed offices. During this time, she served as the Snapchat content producer for the 2016 Olympics in Rio, where she was part of a team that produced content garnering 2.2 billion views and 230 million minutes of consumption.[83]

82 "Grandmas Skydive for the First Time," *BuzzFeed* Video, May 2, 2015, YouTube video, 4:24.

83 "Lizz Warner," LinkedIn, accessed October 7, 2020.

BRING ME!—THE TRAVEL PLATFORM OF OUR GENERATION:

One of the arenas BuzzFeed hadn't fully cracked yet was the travel industry. Lizz decided to take this on headfirst.

"There wasn't a clear go-to website or app to find awesome local places when planning trips. You'd have to find friends of friends who knew of cool spots. My boss at the time told me if I could crack travel (i.e., make it go consistently viral) and at no additional cost compared to regular BuzzFeed videos, he'd help pave the way for me to launch a franchise within BuzzFeed," says Lizz.

Although Lizz hoped a BuzzFeed platform centered around travel would become very popular, she had to experiment and test it out before launch.

"I started shooting content around LA; the first viral video was a cupcake ATM machine at Sprinkles in Beverly Hills. This video shared extremely well, and the next challenge was figuring out how to do this all over the country on an airtight budget," says Lizz.

Lizz and her team created a road trip from LA to Texas where they shot seventy different videos in a week and a half. The videos were very well received, and one of them got over a million shares, which was enough signal to launch the brand. Soon enough, "Bring Me!" was born. Their work eventually took Lizz's crew across the world to locations such as Berlin and the Dominican Republic, bringing their travel experience home to millions of followers.

In less than a year, Bring Me! became the most viewed travel page on Facebook, and the number one global cross-platform travel publisher on the internet.[84] Bring Me! features unique content ranging from cheese road-trip-style documentaries to "5 Things to Do in Vegas If You Hate Vegas."[85]

When Bring Me! started, there were hundreds of different social media platforms launching at the same time. Snapchat, Instagram, and Facebook were already vastly popular amongst millennials, and new platforms were emerging to capture market share.

Lizz highlighted three main reasons why Bring Me! became so successful so quickly:

1. **It was data driven.**
"When we saw content that went viral, we would immediately compare it to other videos, dissect it and analyze why it was performing well," says Lizz. "We then would create hypotheses about why this happened, and continue to iterate based on those successes."

2. **Bring Me! developed content which fit into peoples' core identities**.
Lizz shares, "We wanted to find content people would share with their friends and say, 'this is so me!' or 'this is so you!' Working at BuzzFeed gives you deep-seated knowledge of the most popular core identities, so we would make content targeting those core share statements each time."

---

84 Ibid.
85 "5 Things to Do in Vegas If You Hate Vegas," *BuzzFeed* Video, March 18, 2019, YouTube video, 2:49.

Following this mentality, Bring Me! became a huge platform for phenomenons like eating giant food (huge bowls of ramen), or shops about condoms in Amsterdam.

3. **The creators at Bring Me! followed their gut and intuition in determining which content to feature and how to beat the competition.**

"We soon found ourselves in very heavily saturated market. Other travel publishers would come and feature the same places. We had to constantly innovate, study the data of what did well and what didn't, and make quick decisions based on data and intuition. We were able to find our niche in a way which led us to showcase our experiences in a way other publishers could not." Through following this mentality, Lizz turned Bring Me! into a top travel online publisher.

WORDS OF WISDOM:

Since the start of her career, Lizz has crafted her own unique journey. At BuzzFeed, she created her own opportunities, and this allowed her to pursue a pathway she was very passionate about.

Lizz herself has gone viral for a video she self-produced about going on a Tinder date with an Olympian during the 2018 Olympics in South Korea.[86] The story became so big it made it into the *Korea Herald*. (Spoiler alert: he comes to the BuzzFeed office to surprise her later on.) Currently, Lizz is

---

86 Sam Stryker, Lizz Warner, and Kelly Diamond, "This Girl Matched on Tinder with an Olympic Athlete and Here's What Happened Next," *BuzzFeed*, April 7, 2018.

a content advisor and executive producer on the Biden for President Campaign team.

Lizz credits a great amount of her success to following her intuition: "When you are still learning and figuring out what to do, sometimes you logically reason yourself out of a pathway or a choice you know is right. Women are in tune with their gut feelings and shouldn't squash that away—it is a great power."

Many women in the workplace try to convince themselves a role is not right for them because it falls out of their comfort zone. Through Lizz's personal experiences, she preaches that leaving your comfort zone is often the key to success.

She attributes a great amount of confidence and her "feminist awakening" to *Lean In* by Sheryl Sandberg.[87] Before reading *Lean In,* she was asked once by an interviewer how she had achieved such success. Her response was she was really "lucky."

"After reading *Lean In,* I realized what little credit I gave myself and how often people tried to take it away. But, the power of recognizing systemic flaws is you learn how to work around them. So, I did," says Lizz.

Through encouraging young women to say to themselves, "Wow, I did that," Lizz emphasizes that instead of questioning

---

87 Sheryl Sandberg, *Lean In: Women, Work and the Will to Lead,* (New York: Alfred A. Knopf, 2013).

why something great happens in your life after you work hard, you should own it and remember you deserve it.

Her personal pathway in overcoming Impostor Syndrome is very important for young women who are coined as "The Perfectionist."[88] Think back to the example of Sarah, "The Perfectionist" and digital media consultant who never feels satisfied with her work and constantly strives for "perfection."

In Lizz's personal pathway, she never sought out perfection, nor did she lay out a set plan for any of her projects. Her stories of creating new opportunities like Bring Me! highlight the power of unconventionality, and why embracing the unknown can be so important. Furthermore, Lizz did not follow one approach for her content at Bring Me!. She constantly analyzed the data and adapted her content accordingly.

Women coined as "The Perfectionist" should take Lizz's advice to realize setting out the "perfect plan" or "ideal path" can hinder your creativity in the process.[89] It is possible to be extremely successful in a field without your journey being perfect. In fact, the most successful people learn from imperfections, and use them to build their knowledge.

Through my personal journey in college, one of the biggest trends I have noticed is that many students seek after a specific pathway or set of events that they think will lead them to achieve success. I have found this inhibits students from

---

88 Valerie Young, *The Secret Thoughts of Successful Women: Why Capable People Suffer from the Impostor Syndrome and How to Thrive in Spite of It*, (New York: Crown Business, 2011).

89 Ibid.

using their knowledge to think for themselves and ultimately hinders innovation. If students are constantly trying to follow preexistent pathways or find the most simplistic ways to achieve goals, they will not test their true abilities.

I experienced this when determining what to major in. As a student interested in the financial markets at a school with no undergraduate business school, I initially looked at the major most students pursued while trying to enter the financial services industry: economics. After realizing the economics courses were interesting, but not as applicable to current events as the public policy courses, I decided to major in public policy instead.

I took a less traditional pathway through finance recruiting, but I had unique perspectives on economic policy and Wall Street, which helped me in the interviews. This lesson proved to me unconventional journeys can be just as important as following the status quo, and if you are trying to follow the "perfect path," you are limiting your full potential. It is crucial to follow Lizz's advice and be willing to make mistakes, mold your own pathway, and learn from your past to reach your end goal.

Lizz's drive and positive attitude serve as tremendous momentum for young women entering the media world, and young people starting their careers. Additionally, Lizz's story highlights how in the overarching world of media, content creators have to constantly adapt to the changing market, appealing to users across different platforms, while maintaining an authentic voice. This is ultimately how they can "go viral" and build a unique brand for themselves. These trends are omnipresent amongst popular content creators, particularly on the *Forbes* 30 Under 30 media list.

In addition to Lizz Warner's BuzzFeed story, I also had the opportunity to hear about the iconic rise of the multimedia brand called Betches.

* * *

THE BETCHES HAVE ENTERED THE BUILDING!

I am an avid fan of the multimedia brand, Betches. I can be found scrolling on their Instagram page after a long day of class, reading their hilarious, but relevant, articles while I'm waiting for my nails to dry, and even reading their books while I pretend to jog on the treadmill (key word: pretend). The Betches are there through it all. The founders of Betches showcase what it takes to rise in the modern-day media industry, and they do so with confidence and authenticity. The founders of Betches, also known as the original Betches, made it onto the *Forbes* 30 Under 30 list in media, and their story is truly inspirational.

I had the chance to talk with Sami Fishbein, chief creative officer and co-founder of Betches, to hear the story of Betches firsthand, in addition to any advice she had on becoming a badass woman in the workforce today.

While studying at Cornell, Sami Fishbein, Aleen Kuperman, and Jordana Abraham launched the "Betches Love This" WordPress page from their apartment. As "Betches

Love This" continued to expand and become more popular, it soon became trademarked as just "Betches" in 2015. Since then, Betches has revamped its platform completely. In 2018, Betches turned into a platform not only focusing on relationship advice, college culture, and celebrity gossip, but also incorporating fashion, lifestyle advice, politics, and current events with the same comedic tone established throughout the rest of the site. What started as a dorm room idea turned into an iconic brand that now has over seven million followers, and has expanded into podcasts, live events, newsletters, and books (with two on the *New York Times* best-seller list).

Although the original three founders do not have a distinct or formulaic pathway to their success, they have used innovative approaches to build their brand.

"The three of us came into the startup world with very little connections, and no background degrees in finance or business. We did not have on-point training, but we were all creative, and found ways to navigate the business world," says Sami.

Despite having no experience in the workforce and no background in managing a company, Sami, Aleen, and Jordana maintained true to their mission. These women highlight how it is not necessary to go to business school or meet "minimum requirements" to launch a venture, as long as you are passionate about a mission, and remain focused on your goals.

"When we started Betches we had a lot of fun ideas, but we had to find a focus point. We had to figure out what we were offering, why we were different, and what problem we were trying to solve. There was a lot of trial and error process, but we had to stay clear with what we wanted to achieve, and remain confident in what we knew," says Sami.

Through having a unique focus point, Betches grew rapidly and gained traction in the social media world. From iconic book launch parties, to award-winning voter campaigns, to making it onto the *Forbes* 30 Under 30 list, the founders of Betches are changing the face of social media, and are true embodiments of modern-day female go-getters.

The story of Betches provides valuable lessons for women suffering from Impostor Syndrome. When the founders of Betches began their journey, they had no experience as company leaders and had to essentially figure out how to become CEOs at the age of twenty-three. But, remaining extremely confident in what they knew helped them the entire way.

Think back to the story of Hanna, "The Expert."[90] Hanna initially did not want to apply for a grant seeking out clean water solutions because she did not think she had the knowledge to do something amazing if awarded the grant money.

Instead of hesitating to pursue new opportunities that seemed daunting, the founders of Betches went after them headfirst. They preached that authenticity helped them the entire way, enabling them to stand out within the highly saturated media industry. If Hanna had adapted this mentality, she would

90 Valerie Young, *The Secret Thoughts of Successful Women: Why Capable People Suffer from the Impostor Syndrome and How to Thrive in Spite of It*, (New York: Crown Business, 2011).

have applied to the grant immediately. You have to remind yourself on a daily basis you are capable of success, and that you can bring so much to the table.

The founders of Betches highlight you can still be extremely successful company leaders without having years of experience. They emphasize how important it is to work hard and realize your worth, a valuable lesson for entrepreneurial women.

Similar to Lizz, the founders of Betches never had a playbook, nor tried to establish a distinct plan to reach their goals. Both Lizz and the founders of Betches took unique, game-changing ideas they had and ran with them.

Both Lizz and Sami showcase that, in the constantly changing sphere of social media, powerful women can make it big. It is incredibly important to maintain true to yourself, true to your mission, and remind yourself you are a badass.

KEY TAKEAWAYS:
- Listen to your gut. When you are trying to determine the best next step, or make any decision, the best judge is yourself. You know what's best for yourself.
- If you achieve something great, it is not because you "got lucky." Stop saying that. Own your accomplishments. If someone says, "Wow—you are so successful!" reply with: "Thank you, I've worked really hard!" Trust me on this.
- You do not have to study business, or go to business school, to run a company and/or platform or become

a CEO. Oftentimes you can grow just as much through different work experiences.

- If you see a gap in an industry, or a place where you can add value, go after it. Propose the idea to your boss, tell your mentors about it, or even just work on it independently. If you don't chase after it, who will?

CHAPTER 5

PRODUCING YOUR OWN PATH

———

I distinctly remember my first introduction to the concept of "success," and how this seven-letter word would change my mindset for the rest of my life. Where did this introduction happen? The place where every elementary school child dreams of: a huge dome where students have the opportunity to earn a paycheck, use their very own debit card, and even become the mayor of the town for the day, all while still eating a peanut butter and jelly sandwich with Goldfish crackers for lunch.

Drumroll please…J.A. Biztown.© For those of you who don't know about J.A. Biztown©, it is a simulation of a real-life town where fifth graders are assigned to different jobs, ranging anywhere from store managers, to janitors, to hair salonists, to artists, to everything in between. Long story short, it is the definition of capitalism with a dash of Disney Channel. Terrifying.

At the end of the J.A. Biztown© simulation I attended in fifth grade, everyone gathered around the teachers, and they asked us the question: was everyone successful today? As a fifth grader whose main experience with "success" was being the top scorer of the Cash Cow game on Webkinz, I raised my hand *really* high, watching all of my classmates do the same.

We were each individually called on, recounting why we thought we became successful. One kid named Jack said, "because I made a lot of money." Thank you, Jack, at least you were honest. My friend Tina said, "because I worked with customers all day and helped them." Tina was always a kiss-up, so her response wasn't shocking. When I was called on, my answer fell along the lines of, "I really don't know, but I could do anything I wanted and I actually had control over my life for a change." (I must have been going through the teen angst phase early.)

As much as I would like to look back at this answer and say, "Wow, Barbara...I can't believe you said that," it actually may be one of the smartest things I have ever said. As society instills ideas within the minds of people starting in kindergarten about different perceptions of success, I think it is truly tied to freedom—the freedom to do what you want and have autonomy over your life. Ella Mielniczenko, executive producer at BuzzFeed and *Forbes* 30 Under 30 media star holds a very similar mindset.[91]

---

91   Bruno (HE) Mirchevski, "An Interview with Ella Mielniczenko, Forbes (US & Canada 2019) Media," *Medium*, June 19, 2019.

"I don't have a good definition of success...maybe, freedom is it? The freedom to openly be who I am, to create, to cultivate a life that is balanced. That feels good to me."—Ella Mielniczenko.[92]

Although Ella Mielniczenko and fifth grade Barbara are very different people with very different experiences, they both raise very important questions for young people today. What truly comprises success? Where does success begin? Where does it end? Does it end?

THE RISE OF DIGITAL MEDIA—THE POWER OF CONNECTIVITY:

As the media industry has evolved, digital media has become vastly popular over the past five years. People are communicating in new, innovative ways, and amongst those working in the digital media industry, those who rise to the top are the thinkers whose creative voices shine. People are collaborating via remakes of iconic *Dance Moms* scenes through TikTok, while applying to dream roles through LinkedIn, while even meeting their future Friday night sushi dates on Bumble.

As of 2020, nearly 3.8 million people use social media, and each second eleven people use social media for the first time.[93]

In a world where social media is an instrumental piece of the digital media world, to stand out against other competitors, innovators have to be new, catchy, and original. This is

---

92   Ibid.
93   "Average Time Spent on Social Media (Latest 2020 Data)," Broadband Search.

definitely not an easy task, but Ella Mielniczenko has risen to the challenge.

In a video featured on *Forbes* called "How Ella Mielniczenko's Journey Led Her to Become a Successful Producer at BuzzFeed," Ella shares her career pathway at BuzzFeed, and how her creative voice shines.[94] One of the most fascinating parts of the video is when they depict Ella sharing cocktails with some of her colleagues.

"Many, many of my great ideas come over shared cocktails. A lot of time work doesn't stop at the end of the day. We'll get dinner or we'll get drinks, and we'll keep talking, and we'll keep ideating. Connectivity is very, very important, but as a producer, it's vital," says Ella.[95]

In this video, Ella explains that building your career is not only based on fancy suits and perfect résumés. It is widely attributed to connecting with others and establishing a sense of camaraderie with those who inspire you, and those from whom you can learn.[96]

According to Mark Cuban, multi-billionaire and star of *Shark Tank*, "Watching the best taught me how to run my businesses."[97] Learning from others and connecting with new people builds trust, knowledge, and power.

---

94 Herradura, "How Ella Mielniczenko's Journey Led Her to Become a Successful Executive Producer at BuzzFeed," *Forbes*, November 15, 2019.

95 Ibid.

96 Ibid.

97 "46 Knowledge-packed Mark Cuban quotes on how to stay in business," TheBusinessQuotes.Com, accessed October 5, 2020.

Through interviewing Ella, I had the opportunity to hear firsthand how she manifests connectivity as a producer at a top media company, and how she sets her content apart in the digital media industry.

THE ROOTS OF ELLA'S PASSION FOR FILM:
Growing up in Los Angeles, Ella became very interested in storytelling, filmmaking, and photography. Although her parents did not work in the entertainment industry, she was constantly exposed to collaborative, creative fields in media, which caught her attention early on. Ella enjoyed learning how to shoot and edit videos on her own, and thoroughly enjoyed the personal voice she could share through film. Following her passion, she began taking classes to learn Final Cut Pro, constantly looking for people to collaborate with in the film community.

"From a really young age, I knew I wanted to work in 'film.' Digital media wasn't a thing yet, and neither was social video. Social media was at the very early stages (like MySpace and Live Journal). These spaces felt exciting; they opened up ways to communicate and to share," says Ella.

As social media was beginning to rise, Ella decided to pursue film at Emerson College. There, she learned how to develop and cut film by hand, and gained tremendous insight about the industry she cared so deeply for. Although she thoroughly enjoyed learning about the traditional film industry, she knew digital media would be exploding soon.

"Right when I started college the industry entered a rapid shift with emerging technologies. We didn't know what the future would look like, what jobs would be needed in this new world, and more importantly, we didn't know if what we were learning in school would even be applicable to jobs in the industry," says Ella.

Although Ella knew most of her experience lay in traditional film, she decided entering the digital media world could provide her with a fascinating, new opportunity. After searching for roles combining her interest in video production with this new, rising field, she found a unique opportunity in Buzz-Feed's video department.

BRINGING THE BUZZ TO BUZZFEED—ELLA'S RISE TO THE TOP:

When Ella started at BuzzFeed, it was very new, and there were only a couple of producers. Originally, she only planned to stay at the company for three months. As she saw Buzz-Feed continue to grow, she decided to stay for seven years.

"When you hire a group of young, talented, passionate people and give them space to create, amazing things can happen. BuzzFeed has always been unique in that ideas don't come from the top down. Traditional media takes years to develop projects, but at BuzzFeed we'd come up with an idea, shoot, and edit it, all in one day," says Ella.

The entrepreneurial atmosphere promoted throughout BuzzFeed enabled Ella to launch her own unique ideas and build BuzzFeed's platform even further. Everyone who has

Snapchat knows that when you go to the Discover page, you can find BuzzFeed content ranging from "which new film matches your zodiac sign" to the "steps of determining if you've been ghosted or not."[98] Ella played a huge role in launching BuzzFeed's flagship channel, and she is part of the reason we can see BuzzFeed content on popular apps like Snapchat.

Additionally, Ella helped launch BuzzFeed's first-ever scripted video channel, BuzzFeed Violet. BuzzFeed Violet is a platform where viewers can watch short, relatable films on topics ranging from love, to mental health, to relationships, to other everyday aspects of life.[99] Through establishing the theme these videos are "the good kind of awkward," BuzzFeed Violet attracts the attention of users who can build a sense of community with the characters featured in the videos.[100] Some of these videos include "The 7 Types of People in Your Group Chat," and "12 Clothing Problems," and even "Diet Disaster."[101] Through broadcasting the everyday struggles of millennials, BuzzFeed Violet creates a platform where users feel included and can relate to the content displayed.

Ella also played a huge role in the launch of Pero Like, a unique BuzzFeed platform focused on LatinX content. Pero Like establishes a close-knit community for LatinX viewers, with content ranging from fabulous quinceaneras to comical

---

98 "Ghosting," *BuzzFeed*, accessed October 5, 2020.
99 "BuzzFeed Violet," YouTube, accessed October 5, 2020.
100 Ibid.
101 "BuzzFeed Violet Videos," YouTube, accessed October 5, 2020.

skits about Latino dads.[102] Pero Like is rapidly successful, with over one million YouTube subscribers.[103]

Because Ella's early life was impacted so greatly through storytelling, she now uses the platform of storytelling to build communities and join people together. In a social media world where we are constantly exposed to unrealistic beauty standards and perceptions of the "perfect life," Ella helps to bring in experiences all users can connect to.

FORMING CONNECTIONS FROM THE VERY BOTTOM— ELLA'S TIPS FOR YOUNG PEOPLE IN MEDIA:

Although Ella grew up in Los Angeles, an international center for media and entertainment, she had very few connections entering the media industry. Given these circumstances, Ella constantly tried to meet new people. She believes networking, reaching out, and exiting your comfort zone are some of the key elements of success.

"Ask people to get coffee or lunch so you can ask them about their careers. Don't be afraid to reach out to people over social media or email. Ask questions. Find people in jobs you might want and ask them how they got there. Cultivate a group of peers you can work with and get honest, good, critical feedback from them," says Ella.

In the media industry, forming connections with other people is imperative in hearing about experiences, and determining

---

102 "Pero Like Videos," YouTube, accessed October 5, 2020.
103 Ibid.

which direction you want to go in. When Ella entered the media industry, digital media was new and exciting. Instead of staying away from this sector of media because she did not know much about it, she networked, applied for roles, and sought out advice from others who had already started building careers in this field.

Additionally, Ella highly emphasizes the importance of unconventionality, and why it is okay to sometimes go against the traditional "rules" of the industry you are pursuing.

"Anyone can be a content creator. If you have access to a phone which shoots video, then you are a director. Don't let the traditional rules and guidelines hold you back. Make your art and put it out there. You don't need training or a degree. You just need to have a story to tell and a point of view," says Ella.

In other words, Ella wants anyone and everyone to use whatever platform they have to share their voice. Ella emphasizes that shooting your own video from an iPhone can be just as meaningful as shooting your video in a studio with a full set of camera equipment.

Ella's points about becoming your own director proved true this past year with the explosion of TikTok. As an avid TikTok user, I initially used the app to watch funny clips that would brighten my day. As I continued to explore the app, I saw videos about the best study tips, catchy videos on how to get into law school, and unique videos informing users about current events. These videos came straight from the iPhones of young millennials, and they had thousands of hits.

WHY ELLA'S STORY IS SO IMPORTANT:

Even if you only have five hundred followers on Instagram or thirty followers on TikTok, if you are passionate and want to share your voice, you will be heard. Prior to my interview with Ella, I would have never viewed myself as a "content creator." However, she has shown me that even taping fifteen seconds of myself rambling about my love life drama on TikTok can share my voice and help me build an original platform.

Let's go back to the story I shared about Hanna, "The Expert."[104] Hanna did not apply for a grant initially because she did not check all of the boxes on the requirements list. Once she was convinced to apply, she ended up absolutely crushing the role, proving her initial thoughts wrong.

Ella's story shows how women experiencing thoughts similar to Hanna can overcome them. Rather than shying away from the digital media roles she did not have experience in, Ella applied to them anyways. Instead of backing down due to her lack of experience in the media industry, she reminded herself that she could be a phenomenal content creator because she has a phone that shoots. Furthermore, she overcame her personal challenges by acknowledging that people in the media industry face issues every day, and they need to adapt and learn from them. The learning process is never ending.

"Once you're working and out of school, you'll realize the learning never stops. Take opportunities to learn new skills,

---

104 Valerie Young, *The Secret Thoughts of Successful Women: Why Capable People Suffer from the Impostor Syndrome and How to Thrive in Spite of It*, (New York: Crown Business, 2011).

to learn new technologies, and about new equipment," says Ella.

Instead of slowing your learning process once you have received a job offer or accomplished something great, you should view each new opportunity as a chance to learn.

Something very important Ella mentions is the importance of networking. Reaching out to people via any platform—LinkedIn, email, company website, Insta DMs you name it—can land people jobs, interviews, and life-long connections. According to an article by *Review42*, 85 percent of all positions are filled by networking.[105]

This means that women who want to learn about new positions, shift industries, or nail the interview need to use the network of strong, powerful women around them to their advantage. When drafting a LinkedIn message or email, it is very easy to let your fear of not being intelligent or competent enough get in the way of pressing send. When I first started using LinkedIn, I distinctly remember thinking, "Why would this person who has already finished the recruitment process and landed their job respond to me?"

The truth is: the worst thing that can happen from networking outreach is that someone does not reply, and you wasted a maximum of five minutes crafting an email. It is crucial that young women normalize networking and outreach, so that the stigma of not being an "expert" on a topic doesn't

---

105 Christina Vukova, "73+ Surprising Networking Statistics to Boost Your Career," *Review42*, February 20, 2020.

get in the way. Ella used the power of networking and out-reach each step of her career path, and I used it to finish this book. Without the power of Instagram DM or LinkedIn free trials, I would not have had nearly as many interviews from incredible women.

Ella continues to shape the face of media through her unique, creative content, and her story is one that can resonate with people entering careers in any industry. Ella is now engaged to Hannah Hart, the founder of My Drunk Kitchen, and plans on continuing to build her voice in digital media.

KEY TAKEAWAYS:
- In the current social media market, anyone can be a content creator. If you have a phone that records, you have the ability to share your voice and story.
- Normalize cold-calls and cold-emails. It is the twenty-first century, and the reality of networking is that you will not always know the person you are reaching out to. Take a chance, and send the email or DM. Even after you have landed a job, keep networking and building connections. The learning cycle should never stop.
- Even if you are a young person at a company, or just starting your role, speak up if you have an innovative idea. Young talent is instrumental for a company's success.

CHAPTER 6

FROM BACKSTAGE TO THE FRONT PAGE

———

Imagine it is a hot, summer afternoon. You just received a call from Mark Holgate, a top editor from the internationally renowned *Vogue* magazine. He asks if you are interested in sitting down with Anna Wintour, the editor-in-chief of *Vogue* magazine, to interview for a fashion-writer position.[106] Anna Wintour is the queen of the fashion industry, and one of the most iconic figures in the world—OMG.

You begin to prepare nonstop. First of all, you need to figure out what you're going to wear. It has to be memorable, yet sophisticated. Fashionable, but not too outspoken. You settle for a cream Michael Kors shift dress from his latest collection.[107]

---

106 Amy Odell, "My Job Interview with Anna Wintour," *New York Post*, August 30, 2015.
107 Ibid.

The time has come for the interview and you reach the twelfth floor of the building: *Vogue*'s chambers. All you can think is *Don't fall in the heels. Don't vomit. Don't stain the Kors. You can do this.*[108]

You walk into Anna's office and it feels just like a scene from *The Devil Wears Prada*. The abnormally long walk to Anna's desk seems like it could have come right out of the movie itself. She stares down your outfit, shakes your hand, and begins to ask the typical, generic interview questions.[109]

Soon enough, hobbies are brought up. You mention you enjoy running, and you love visiting your boyfriend at Harvard Business School in your free time.[110] You wanted to prove you were in shape, but also had connections to a place prestigious socialites used in their everyday conversations.

Then, Anna asks if you've been to any museums lately. Museums? Why does she care about that?[111] You answer that you enjoy museums, and then she asks which exhibits you've recently seen. You tell her you're excited about an upcoming *Vogue* exhibit at the Spanish Institute but can't come up with anything else.[112]

---

108 Ibid.
109 Ibid.
110 Ibid.
111 Ibid.
112 Ibid.

After a few other questions, Anna quickly says, "Lovely to see you," staring you up and down, and you are dismissed from her chamber.[113]

A couple of days later, you receive a rejection e-mail stating you did not get the position.[114]

You may be wondering, what happens now? Do I end up going into seclusion and dismiss myself from the fashion world altogether?

The answer is absolutely not. This story is a shortened, but very similar account from Amy Odell's book titled *Tales from the Back Row: An Outsider's View from Inside the Fashion Industry*.[115] Although Amy's interview with Anna Wintour seems terrifying, it was, interestingly enough, an instrumental part of her career.

Amy Odell is a major figure in the media industry known for her transformative roles at *New York Magazine*'s fashion blog, The Cut, BuzzFeed, and as the former editor of Cosmpolitan. com. Amy was named on the *Forbes* 30 Under 30 list for media, and her work has revolutionized women's media in many different ways. Amy is particularly known for her role in transforming Cosmpolitan.com into a site that focuses on women's rights and current events, in addition to its normal content on fashion, sex, and celebrity gossip. Amy created an authentic, unique voice for herself through creativity and

---

113 Ibid.
114 Ibid.
115 Ibid.

perseverance, and has truly changed the norms of media content for women.

I had the opportunity to interview Amy and hear the story of how she made it in one of the most highly saturated markets of the world.

FROM BEHIND THE RED CARPET TO TOP OF THE HEADLINES:

As a young girl, Amy was always interested in the media and news world. In an interview with her own website, Cosmopolitan.com, she talked about watching Barbara Walters on TV, and always looking up to her.[116]

Amy's strong drive, phenomenal work ethic, and desire for her own New York City *Sex and the City* experience led her to NYU, where she studied journalism. Living in one of the fashion capitals of the world, Amy decided to pursue fashion even though she knew it would be difficult to break into.

One of the first positions Amy held was freelancing for *New York Magazine.* In this role, she went to tons of celebrity parties and red-carpet events. Her editors wanted her to report very specific stories about recent celebrity news, and if she didn't abide by their guidelines, she was taken off events.

In Amy's interview with Cosmopolitan.com, she spoke about interviewing Kurt Loder on her first assignment.[117] After she

---

116 Heather Wood Rudolph, "Get That Life: How I Became the Editor of Cosmopolitan.com," *Cosmopolitan.com*, August 31, 2015.

117 Ibid.

interviewed him, the editor sent out a mass email asking for new people to report at parties. Amy reached back out and said, "Look, I went out for you once before and you didn't like what I filed. But I know that I'm good. I know I can do this, and I really want to go out for you again."[118] After standing her ground, Amy was able to continue reporting at parties. Amy's determination in this situation helped her become more confident and learn from her mistakes.

After working as a party reporter for *New York Magazine*, continuously building content, and gaining publicity in the press, Amy was offered a unique position: to jumpstart the fashion segment of *New York Magazine*.

At only twenty-two years old, Amy started The Cut, a platform where she could write blog posts about fashion but also share her feminist perspectives with the world. After four years at The Cut, Amy accepted a role at BuzzFeed as they were trying to expand their female audience. Following a brief period at BuzzFeed, Amy received the offer of a lifetime: to become editor of the entire Cosmpolitan.com platform.

TALK DIRTY TO ME...BUT ALSO TALK NERDY TO ME— AMY'S TRANSFORMATION OF COSMOPOLITAN.COM:
When Amy started as editor of Cosmopolitan.com, most sites that directly targeted women did not cover sex, fashion, and relationships, in addition to politics and current events. There was not a single place where women could read about

---

118 Ibid.

celebrity hookup stories, while also learning about upcoming elections and tax reform. When Troy Young, former president of Hearst Digital Media, asked her to become the editor of Cosmopolitan.com, he wanted Amy to transform its platform. Of course, keeping some sex talk and celebrity gossip was important (this was how the original founder of *Cosmopolitan* gained traction, after all).[119] But, the leaders at *Cosmopolitan* wanted it to become a new media source for women where they could get everything they needed in one place.[120]

"I feel like a lot of articles for women were written in a very dumbed-down way, and I didn't understand why it was like this. I wanted to make sure Cosmopolitan.com did not use juvenile language, and this is what drove the editorial mission," says Amy.

Following this approach, Cosmopolitan.com brought greater awareness to topics like sexual assault, politics, and current events. In an interview with *Fashion Week Daily*, Amy spoke further about how *Cosmo*'s new brand became vastly popular amongst millennials.

"It's such an exciting time to be a women's brand in particular because there are so many things going on—the Harvey Weinstein story came out, the #MeToo movement, sexual harassment stories, and the upcoming midterm elections. Some of the most-shared stories on *Cosmo*...were about the

---

119 Ibid.
120 Ibid.

tax plan being terrible. That would not have been the case when I started," says Amy.[121]

Through Amy's leadership, Cosmopolitan.com's traffic tripled to thirty-six million monthly visitors.[122] After four-and-a-half years, she decided to step down from her role. In a letter to the *Cosmo* staff, Amy expressed how proud she was for expanding *Cosmo*'s scope to advance political, feminist, and LGBTQ+ topics. Some of the highlights she referenced included an interview with Ivanka Trump, and a guide on how to run for office.[123]

Now, Amy is working on her second book, and she works as a digital journalist and media consultant while living in Westchester with her son and husband.

DON'T TAKE REJECTIONS PERSONALLY:
After interviewing Amy and reading about her life, I was absolutely amazed. With hardly any connections, she succeeded in a world that was incredibly hard to break into. But, don't get me wrong; she faced many challenges along the way and constantly had to prove herself.

When I asked Amy what advice she would give young women, she emphasized the importance of hard work. She stressed that so many of her accomplishments have come from

121 Ashley Baker, "Amy Odell Knows Why Your Digital Media Brand Is Failing," *The Daily Front Row*, February 12, 2018.
122 Ibid.
123 Emilia Petrarca, "Cosmopolitan.com Editor Steps Down," *The Cut*, January 25, 2018.

working extremely hard, and from building herself back up whenever she faced doubt.

This was the mentality she followed after being rejected from her dream job at *Vogue*, and after doing a subpar job on the reporting gig for the *New York Magazine*. When Amy saw that her editor at the *New York Magazine* was trying to find new people for the reporting role, she told them, "I can, and I will do better."

An issue I have noticed that many young women face is that they are immediately discouraged after a single rejection or a wrong turn in their trajectory. This happened to me in my first semester at Duke when I took Math 111. After thinking I was strong at math based on my high school performance, I completely struggled with the theoretical way Duke math was taught.

Instead of dropping the course, I adapted to the new style of teaching, outlined the material in new ways, and ultimately ended up on a first-name basis with every single tutor in the math help room. Instead of questioning why I wasn't performing as well as expected, I acknowledged I would have to put in greater effort to get a good grade. This mentality ultimately helped me succeed, and enabled me to view the unexpected turns in life from a new lens.

It is 2020, and it is time to normalize failure and the unexpected turns in life. There is no path that is truly perfect; young people who seek perfection will face failure at some point or, quite frankly, live extremely boring lives.

Amy's story offers young women valuable knowledge on ways to combat obstacles in the workplace such as Impostor Syndrome.

Think back to the story of Sarah, "The Perfectionist."[124] "The Perfectionist" embodies the person who will not stop working until they think they have reached perfection.[125] This is the issue so many women in the workplace face. They want to work hard and be proud of their work, but they go overboard in the process. It is extremely difficult to find the balance between working hard, and working too hard, and it feels like there is no way to reach this median. Although it is very difficult to find balance, Amy offers valuable insight on this process.

Amy found balance in her career by owning up to the accomplishments she was proud of. Instead of working nonstop, she took time to reflect.

When Amy left Cosmopolitan.com, she shared insight about her personal decision with *The Daily Front Row.*

"I felt like I conquered it, and I'm really proud of the work I did there, and I'm ready for my next challenge. I want to find ways to learn new things," says Amy.[126]

---

124 Valerie Young, *The Secret Thoughts of Successful Women: Why Capable People Suffer from the Impostor Syndrome and How to Thrive in Spite of It,* (New York: Crown Business, 2011).

125 Ibid.

126 Ashley Baker, "Amy Odell Knows Why Your Digital Media Brand Is Failing," *The Daily Front Row,* February 12, 2018.

Rather than striving to "perfect" Cosmopolitan.com, Amy acknowledged that the work she had done there was amazing and truly impactful for female readers across the globe. Amy emphasizes that you must acknowledge when you have done well in a role, rather than continuing to work yourself unnecessarily. Owning your accomplishments and maintaining a work-life balance is incredibly important.

Christine Louise Hohlbaum, author and public relations professional, introduced a fascinating perspective on work-life balance that has truly resonated with me. According to Hohlbaum, "We get into trouble when we treat our work lives as polar opposites to our personal lives. In today's world, we blend both and should embrace that. Work-life balance is really about being in alignment with your truest purpose and making choices based on that purpose."[127]

Following Hohlbaum's advice, I try to create a fluid schedule where I have time to relax and work. In my personal schedule for studying, I create short breaks of at least thirty minutes for every three hours I spend studying. This can be a coffee break, phone call with a friend, loop around the Duke chapel—basically anything other than studying. I try to relax at least one sixth of the time I spend working or studying.

Ambitious people with high aspirations need to stay focused, but staying focused also requires practicing good health, both inside and out. Hard-working people need to take breaks and

---

127 Margarita Tartakovsky, "How Experts Achieve a Work-Life Balance and How You Can Too," *PsychCentral*, October 8, 2018.

have time to reflect. Without periods of self-reflection, Amy would not be where she is today.

Amy's story highlights the importance of taking leaps of faith, but also working your butt off in the process. She serves as a strong role model for women in media all over the world, and all young people can come one step closer to reaching their personal version of success through following her advice.

Read it and weep, Anna Wintour.

KEY TAKEAWAYS:
- Even if a new role seems daunting, if it fits into your over-all mission, go after it. New roles can help you build new skills, and grow as an innovator.
- If you produce something that isn't necessarily your best work, leave the past behind. Tell your boss you can and will do better, and acknowledge your mistakes.
- Self-reflection and short breaks are incredibly important for growth. If you do not reflect on what you've done well, and allow yourself to build back positive energy, you will not have an effective growth mindset.

CHAPTER 7

BABY FEVER

It's the night of the Superbowl in 2009. You have no idea who is playing, but of course, you grab your chips, guacamole, and mini sliders because it is time for the best part: the half-time commercials. Suddenly, a baby appears on the screen and starts talking about an electronic trading platform. Everyone in your family looks confused, but honestly, whatever is going on is really entertaining. The baby is legitimately speaking like a grown adult in a child's body. He is talking about his experience on electronic trading platforms, straight from a webcam in his nursery.[128] Iconic.

This moment was the entrepreneurial spark that branded E-Trade and projected its image onto the general public.[129] Although this commercial was about electronic trading and brokerage accounts, it made me question: why is the concept of a baby speaking so abstract? At what point do babies actually understand what's going on? How were my language skills actually acquired growing up?

---

128 *Wall Street Journal*, "ETrade 'Baby' Super Bowl Ad," February 1, 2013, YouTube video, 0:18.

129 Ibid.

Although I can't imagine that the marketing team at E-Trade intended to spark my deep thought process about language acquisition and speaking development, this is exactly what happened.

Growing up in Charlotte, North Carolina while my parents were at work, my grandmother spent most of the day with me speaking predominately in Greek. By the time I was three years old, I could compile Greek words into sentences, and by the time I was six years old, I could speak, read, and write Greek fluently. When I entered middle school, I took Spanish courses as electives. I continued Spanish lessons for four years in high school, but I cannot say I am fluent by any means. I can speak Spanish somewhat conversationally, write a five-paragraph essay, and conjugate the present, past, and future-verb tenses. But, if you stuck me in a Spanish-speaking country alone, that would really not end well. If you studied with me in Europe, you know what I'm talking about—*la discoteca* is *very* different than the grocery store.

While reflecting on my different language experiences, I learned that the later in life I start learning a language, the more difficult it becomes. This has always been a hard concept for me to grasp. According to the *TIME* article "Why It's So Hard to Learn Another Language After Childhood," possible explanations why the drop-in learning ability happens at the threshold of adulthood include "changes in brain plasticity, lifestyle changes related to entering the workforce of college…[and] an unwillingness to learn new things—potentially while looking foolish—that mounts with age."[130]

Although there are some explanations surrounding how age affects language acquisition and development, scientist Elika Bergelson is revolutionizing the way this type of research is taking place. Dr. Elika Bergelson was selected for the *Forbes* 30 Under 30 list in the science sector for her work in cognitive development and language acquisition research. In addition to being named to the *Forbes* 30 Under 30 list, Elika received the Steve Reznick Early Career Award from the Cognitive Development Society, and her work has been funded by sources like the Early Independence Award from the National Institutes for Health.

I had the opportunity to speak with Elika and gain greater insight about her experiences as a woman in research to discover why she chose a path studying language and development.

CHILDHOOD QUESTIONS CAN SPARK CAREER PATHWAYS:

Elika grew up in Columbus, Ohio, with three sisters, a brother, and two parents from Russia. Both of her parents were born in Russia, then emigrated to Israel in the 1970s, and ultimately emigrated to Ohio in the 1980s. In Elika's home growing up, everyone spoke Russian, and her older siblings

---

130 Jamie Ducharme, "Why It's So Hard to Learn Another Language after Childhood," *Time*, May 2, 2018.

also spoke Hebrew. In this environment, Elika immediately noticed her English and her parents' English differed.

"I got to wondering how it was my parents and I had both been learning English for about the same amount of time, but with pretty different outcomes. They both have excellent English, but it's clear they're not native English speakers," says Elika.

Elika also noticed her older sisters who moved to the United States as young children were readily able to quickly switch from Russian and Hebrew to English. Through her family experiences growing up, Elika wanted to learn more about cognitive development and the language learning process.

After high school, Elika took every opportunity possible to conduct research, and to learn more about the intersection between cognitive development and linguistics. For her undergraduate career, Elika attended NYU, where she studied language and mind, music, and French. After graduating from NYU, she held a research fellowship at the University of Maryland, and ultimately pursued her PhD at the University of Pennsylvania. Prior to becoming a professor at Duke University, Elika was a researcher at the University of Rochester for three years. At Rochester, Elika served as the principal investigator of a longitudinal study called SEEDLingS (Study of Environmental Effects on Developing Linguistic Skills). Elika is currently the head of the Bergelson Lab (BLAB) which is a part of the Child and Infant Learning and Development (CHILD) Studies Group. The main goal of the Bergelson Lab is to "study infant word learning, in particular how infants' early linguistic and environmental input plays a role in their learning." After moving to Duke University, Elika continued to carry out the SEEDLingS study in the BLAB.[131]

INNOVATIVE WAYS ELIKA IS ASSESSING COGNITIVE DEVELOPMENT:

Dr. Bergelson is an example of a game-changer who uses her curiosities about the world to seek answers and pursue studies that have never been conducted before.

One example of a research method Elika has used to assess cognitive development of babies is combining lab-based measures like eye tracking with measures of babies' home environments.[132]

During the eye tracking trials, Elika brings baby subjects into the lab. They sit on their parent's lap in front of a special computer with an eye tracking camera at the bottom. During these trials, research analysts show the babies pictures or videos on a screen, then tell them a sentence saying to look at a specific picture or video.

For example, babies might see a picture of a hand and some yogurt and hear a sentence like "Look at the yogurt!"

Then, the computer and camera automatically measure where the babies look. Elika and her research analysts then use this information to determine which words the babies understood.

131 Nadia Bey, "Elika Bergelson wins early career award for child linguistic development research," *Duke Chronicle*, December 3, 2019.
132 "Elika Bergelson," Bergelson Lab, accessed July 5, 2020.

From these types of eye tracking experiments, Dr. Bergelson discovered that at six months, babies do a better job telling apart unrelated words than related words.[133] Although these are only the preliminary results of Dr. Bergelson's study, they are strongly indicative of her hard work in understanding cognitive development.

In the future, Elika plans on continuing to learn about the basic science of language development, how babies learn language, and how language learning relates to babies' cognitive and social development more broadly.

BUILDING UPON THE STRONG FEMALE FOUNDATION IN COGNITIVE DEVELOPMENT RESEARCH:

As a woman in the overarching world of research, Elika is a minority.

According to UNESCO, only 30 percent of the world's researchers are women.[134] In the United States, the percentage of female researchers is only slightly better. According to an article from the American Association for the Advancement of Science, the average ratio of female to male researchers ranges from 40 percent to 44 percent in the United States.[135]

---

133 Will Boggs, "Babies learn what words mean before they can use them," *Reuters*, November 20, 2017.

134 "Just 30% of the world's researchers are women. What's the situation in your country?" UNESCO.

135 Rachel Bernstein, "More female researchers globally, but challenges remain," *Sciencemag.org*, March 9, 2017.

UNESCO also reports that female researchers tend to work in academic and government sectors, and are very poorly represented in the private research sectors, where there are tremendous salary and growth opportunities.[136] Examples of private sector research include being on an R&D team for a pharmaceutical company, or working on research for an engineering firm. Beyond the fact that females are not represented as highly within the overall realm of research in the United States, female researchers do not have as many opportunities for salary and career advancement as their male counterparts.

It is clear there needs to be greater representation of women in research overall, and that women currently in research roles need equitable opportunities for support.

Female representation in research continues to worsen as women reach the mid-career gap. According to the "Parents in Science" study led by Erin Cech, a sociologist at the University of Michigan in Ann Arbor, "more than 40 percent of women with full-time jobs in science leave the sector or go part time after having their first child."[137] This means as women become scientists and research experts, they face an impediment in the middle of their careers if they plan on starting families. Due to these circumstances, fewer female researchers become published.

---

136 "Just 30% of the world's researchers are women. What's the situation in your country?" UNESCO.

137 Holly Else, "Nearly half of US female scientists leave full-time science after first child," *Nature.com*, February 19, 2020.

When I asked Elika about the underrepresentation of women in STEM pathways, particularly research, she responded with a surprising yet encouraging answer.

"Language acquisition research, and cognitive development research are actually funny subfields—while psychology and neuroscience more broadly do have gender imbalance, our little subfield has long had quite strong female representation. This is of course in part because babies are often associated with women, but the nice side effect is lots of seminal work in our field has been done by strong female scholars for decades," says Elika.

Due to the strong foundation other female researchers have established in cognitive development and language acquisition research, Elika plans to continue to build upon the phenomenal work already in place.

WHAT IS THE BIG PICTURE OF ELIKA'S PATHWAY?

When I asked Elika for advice she would give to young women interested in research, or young women pursuing male-dominated fields, she emphasized the importance of perseverance: "My advice to young women is that trailblazing is hard, but don't get shut out of what you're doing just because no one around you looks like you. Persist!"

Elika stresses that when things get tough or when you lack motivation, it is important to persist and remind yourself you have the ability to achieve great things. It is also extremely important to reach out to your support network. Female mentors can help you stay motivated and keep your head in the game. Odds are they have faced very similar obstacles to the ones you are currently facing.

According to Ara Wilson, associate professor of gender, sexuality, and feminist studies, "having a senior woman scientist mentor junior scientists is a good step toward remedying the historical favoritism of men in the field...having students see laboratories staffed by women scientists helps to transform the presumption that one gender is more naturally at home in the sciences."[138] As a professor at Duke University teaching a course called "Cognitive Development," Elika is serving the part as a senior mentor extremely well.

One of the greatest issues women face in their careers is feeling like they do not have what it takes to make an impact. For women who are trailblazing in highly male-dominated industries, this trend is unfortunately common. This is one of the detrimental traits of Impostor Syndrome. Think back to the story of Hanna, "The Expert."[139] Although Hanna spent many years of her life researching clean water solutions, she did not think she had the capability to develop a viable clean water solution if she was awarded grant money. One way to break free from this mindset is to interact with mentors, and to remind yourself of everything you have already accomplished.

---

138 Nadia Bey, "Elika Bergelson wins early career award for child linguistic development research," *Duke Chronicle*, December 3, 2019.

139 Valerie Young, *The Secret Thoughts of Successful Women: Why Capable People Suffer from the Impostor Syndrome and How to Thrive in Spite of It*, (New York: Crown Business, 2011).

Elika is considered an expert in the field of cognitive development, but she uses each new opportunity to expand her knowledge. Additionally, she now mentors young women so they can also maximize their potential. Instead of succumbing to internal doubts or challenges, Elika recognizes the breakthroughs she has made, and continues to build upon them. Through contributing to the mentorship cycle, Elika helps even more women break free from Impostor Syndrome.

KEY TAKEAWAYS:
- Contribute to the mentorship cycle. Use your mentors to your advantage, and mentor younger people when you can. The mentorship cycle helps women collaborate, and grow as leaders.
- Don't exit from fields or industries just because you are different than the majority. You have the ability to trailblaze and make an impact.
- The questions and observations you grow up with can drive your career path. Stay curious and always ask questions.

CHAPTER 8

TRANSFORMING THE WORLD OF CLEAN ENERGY

———

Imagine waking up in the blazing heat surrounded by unpaved roads, no electricity, and straw huts where you are helping to raise your four siblings—the youngest of whom just turned two years old. While your brothers head to work for the day, it is your duty to gather water for the family. You hastily begin the trek, walking in your long sari carrying three huge containers. After walking for six miles straight, you gather the water and head back home for another six-mile trek, this time, with all of the containers filled to the rim. Once the sun goes down, you can finally rest for the night, until 6 a.m. when the cycle starts all over again.

This is the reality many women face in the villages of India and Pakistan, where resources like safe drinking water, energy, and transportation are completely uncertain. Almost one-fifth of the entire world's population without access to clean water lives in India.[140] Over 163 million people in India lack access to clean water and fight for their everyday survival.[141] In Pakistan, over twenty-one million people lack access to clean water, ranking them number nine in the list of top ten countries with lowest access to clean water.[142]

When young Arsheen Allam traveled with her family to their home countries of India and Pakistan, her parents made a point to take her and her sisters, who were born and raised in North America, on road trips to impoverished regions. In these areas, she immediately noticed enormous disparities between her living conditions in Canada and the living conditions present. While she could access clean water safely from her refrigerator with the touch of a button, or even her tap, locals here had to travel great distances to access water, not knowing whether or not it would be clean or safe. After seeing firsthand how certain parts of the world had very limited access to the resources Arsheen had access to in her everyday life, she sought change.

Arsheen Allam is the founder of CNanoz, a company that produces nanotech-based carbon water filters, and GOLeafe, a company developing cheaper graphene derivatives for use in both water desalination and energy applications. Arsheen made it onto the *Forbes* 30 Under 30 list in the energy sector. When I had the opportunity to interview Arsheen, she told me about her pathway in founding two start-ups before age

---

140 Kiran Pandey and Rajit Sengupta, "19% of world's people without access to clean water live in India," *DownToEarth*, March 23, 2018.

141 Ibid.

142 Sana Jamal, "21 million in Pakistan don't have access to clean water: report," *GulfNews*, March 22, 2018.

thirty, and how she plans to transform the clean water and clean energy spheres.

TRIPS TO THE HOMELAND—ARSHEEN'S PATHWAY IN FOUNDING TWO START-UPS:

When Arsheen expanded upon her childhood, she spoke about the trips to her parents' homelands, and how shocking conditions in certain parts of India and Pakistan were.

"Because I grew up in the West, seeing so many people without access to basic necessities like energy and clean water really shook me," says Arsheen.

After obtaining firsthand exposure to the conditions present, she found her mission: democratizing access to clean water and energy, which was in large part due to her Muslim faith. In line with one of Islam's five pillars of giving to charity and alleviating pains of the less fortunate, Arsheen wanted to contribute to the livelihood of society in any way she could. While determining what to study in college, she knew she wanted to pursue a career that would leave a positive impact on underserved communities.

"I wanted to study something that would lead to change," says Arsheen.

With hopes to improve the structural flaws in India and Pakistan's clean water and energy systems, Arsheen decided to pursue a major in materials science and engineering from North Carolina State University.

While at NC State, Arsheen learned the importance of economies of scale in creating viable products, especially in price-sensitive markets. She spent a large amount of her time in her undergraduate experience working on a research project to develop low-cost water filters, and during her senior year she filed a patent for these water filters.

After patenting these water filters, Arsheen founded CNanoz, a nanotechnology-based company focused on developing water purification solutions. CNanoz began doing business in India, supplying carbon nano filters to places ranging from schools and orphanages to hotels and large water plants.[143]

"While running CNanoz, I learned carbon filtration worked for groundwater and river water, but not saltwater. Because most of Earth's water is in the oceans, I wanted to find a desalination solution," says Arsheen.

This led Arsheen to learning about "wonder material" graphene, which according to a publication by MIT at the time, claimed to be the most promising water desalination solution. Arsheen then dove into research on graphene and how to extract it in a more efficient and eco-friendly way. In the process, she determined this material would be a great source for clean energy products as well. So, she began to experiment. After successfully extracting graphene from different carbon sources, Arsheen filed a patent for her production process, and sought to find unique ways graphene could be used. Thus, GOLeafe was born.

---

143 "Arsheen Allam." *The Business Journals.*

The GOLeafe team is working to solve the issue of graphene being extremely expensive to produce. Through their proprietary, patent-pending production process using low-cost source and input materials in place of harsh chemicals and energy-intensive equipment, GOLeafe's graphene products are cheaper, scalable, and eco-friendly.

Arsheen wants to use graphene to grant underserved populations access to clean water and electricity in an affordable, eco-friendly way. Through the GOLeafe platform, she is tackling several important issues at the same time.

Currently, Arsheen has developed three different proof of concept products: 1) a water desalination membrane, 2) a supercapacitor/energy storage device, and 3) a solar panel. GOLeafe is now seeking strategic partners and potential investors to further develop these prototypes and eventually commercialize the promising products.

In an interview with *Thrive Global*, Arsheen stated her ultimate dream is "to create a self-sustaining desalination unit—one that uses graphene as both the power source as well as the filtration technology."[144] Arsheen wants this unit to serve underprivileged communities so they can have reliable sources of water and power, independent of grid or municipal infrastructure. Slowly but surely, Arsheen is solving many of the issues she observed on her family trips.

---

144 Christina Warner, "Big Ideas with Founder and CEO of GOLeafe Arsheen Allam," *Thrive Global*, May 2, 2019.

OVERCOMING CHALLENGES AS A YOUNG, FEMALE ENTREPRENEUR:

Arsheen Allam has launched two start-ups in areas she is passionate about, and both are tracking to be very successful. I asked Arsheen about struggles she may have faced along the way and how she overcame them.

"Finding the right partner, whether it is an investor or a commercial partner, can be very difficult. I have been working on my research for ten years now, and I want to ensure the people I introduce to the company are mutually beneficial to my mission," says Arsheen.

In an interview with *Thrive Global,* Arsheen also talks about how important humility is.[145] In one particular situation, Arsheen fired the wrong employee when productivity was down.[146] She held one-on-one meetings with all team members and thought she knew who was the root cause of the problem.[147] Soon, she realized she had made a mistake.[148] Turns out there was a different employee taking credit for the work the quieter, hard-working person was doing.[149] Arsheen then had to call the woman she had fired and admit her mistake, ultimately asking if the woman would be willing to return. The woman has been with Arsheen's team ever since.[150]

---

145 Ibid.
146 Ibid.
147 Ibid.
148 Ibid.
149 Ibid.
150 Ibid.

Having to fix this situation was a significant obstacle Arsheen faced in her career, but it taught her an important lesson on humility: it is not only perfectly okay, but admirable to admit you have done something wrong. This is an important concept people working in all industries need to understand. I have learned from my own personal experiences you must showcase your abilities confidently, but do so in an open-minded and respectful manner. For example, if you figure out the answers to a coding issue while working in a group project, telling the group what you have accomplished is great. But, if you begin to boast and criticize your group members for not solving the code as fast as you, the group dynamic will be ruined.

FINDING A PASSION, AND GOING FOR IT:

When I asked Arsheen for advice she would give to young women, she emphasized the importance of being passionate about your mission, and "having your village." For Arsheen, her village started with her parents. Her parents constantly supported her and her dreams.

"If you want to be an entrepreneur, you need to make sure it is for something you really care about. If you're not passionate enough about it, the self-doubt you naturally feel as a young entrepreneur will eventually get the best of you," says Arsheen.

Through exposing the realities of entrepreneurship, Arsheen makes it clear even when you have a set mission, it is still definitely not easy, but at least you are putting yourself out there to make the world a better place.

Because I used a Mark Cuban quote earlier in the book, it is only right I bring up his badass co-star, famous entrepreneur, and venture investor, Lori Greiner. Lori always offers insightful advice on *Shark Tank* but, in my opinion, one of her most impactful quotes is, "As an entrepreneur, you can always find a solution if you try hard enough."[151]

From my experience in college, it is clear the greatest fear young people have when pursuing new ideas or concepts is rejection or the fear they will not accomplish their goal immediately. Instead of propagating the fear of failure amongst young people, Lori exemplifies any person can solve a problem through entrepreneurship; you just have to be willing to put in the work.

While tackling the world of finding clean water and energy solutions, Arsheen did not back down from the challenge. She knew she had to work very hard and intelligently to become successful.

NOT ALL ENTREPRENEURS ARE EXTROVERTS:
In addition to finding passion behind entrepreneurship, Arsheen spoke to me about a fascinating misconception within society: the idea all entrepreneurs are extroverts. She emphasized that young women who are more introverted should not shy away from entrepreneurship because she is more introverted herself.

---

151 Brian Ainsley Horn, "10 Quotes from Lori Greiner That Will Make You Proud to Be an Entrepreneur," *Authority Alchemy.*

A *Medium* article titled, "10 of the Most Common Entrepreneurship Myths," states "entrepreneurs may be gregarious extroverts or quiet; they may be 'big picture' thinkers or more focused on the details of executing an idea."[152] The fact that the author of this article had to outline entrepreneurs are not always extroverted shows how grand this misconception is within American society.

I originally believed this misconception as well until I began college. As a student in an innovation and entrepreneurship program, I have had the opportunity to meet many different entrepreneurs and start-up employees. Some of them are the most outgoing people I have met in my entire life, while others are more reserved. This does not impact their success; however, they have each individually found ways to advance their careers and build their paths.

In a *Forbes* article titled, "How Introverts Can Thrive as Entrepreneurs," Caroline Castrillon references J.K. Rowling, Bill Gates, and Mark Zuckerberg as famous introverts who are extremely successful entrepreneurs. Castrillon references a study where analysts examined the personalities of two thousand CEOs for ten years.[153] Once this study was completed, analysts found the vast majority of the successful entrepreneurs were actually introverts.[154]

---

152 Keith Krach, "10 of the Most Common Entrepreneurship Myths," *Medium.com*, May 23, 2017.

153 Caroline Castrillon, "How Introverts Can Thrive as Entrepreneurs," *Forbes*, January 23, 2019.

154 Ibid.

Arsheen spoke about how being an introvert did not negatively impact her in her pathway. Additionally, Arsheen expressed that being the CEO of a company has taught her so much about herself and how important networking can be.

"At first, I dreaded phone introductions, and didn't want to take them. But over time I realized how important they were. I'm so grateful for new connections I have made because they have helped me discover many new ideas and concepts. At the end of the day, people take networking calls with you because they are interested in what you are doing, and this can lead to an array of new opportunities," says Arsheen.

As an introvert, Arsheen learned to appreciate networking, even if it caused her to leave her comfort zone. She believes this is an important skill that young women pursuing entrepreneurship should use to their advantage. Even as a seasoned entrepreneur, Arsheen says half-jokingly, "I still break a sweat at the thought of entering a networking event, with a room full of bright strangers. Now that all of my networking meetings are via Zoom, due to the pandemic, I often still get nervous when turning on my camera."

WHY ARSHEEN'S PATH IS SO IMPORTANT:
After seeing firsthand the conditions in our world she wanted to change, Arsheen sought solutions. Arsheen pursued clean water and energy, she studied materials science extensively, and she launched two different start-ups to support her mission. Due to Arsheen's contributions, people in underprivileged communities are one step closer to having access to clean water and electricity.

Along the way, Arsheen has continued to search for innovative solutions while learning to trust others in the process. After seeing the issues present in our world, Arsheen worked to grow her knowledge base rather than back down from the challenge.

When it comes to major issues in the world, many women in the workplace suffering from Impostor Syndrome do not believe they have the capability to solve them. Some think to themselves, "Who am I to think I can solve something so grand, like the lack of access to clean water in so many parts of the world?"

Often times while presenting her research and the solutions she has developed at large, national technology conferences like IDTechEx and TechConnect, Arsheen found herself being one of the youngest, one of the only women, the *only* presenter without a PhD, and the only visibly Muslim person on the stage. This would give her the feeling of Impostor Syndrome. Initially, this led to Arsheen ignoring or declining speaker invitations even before learning more details about the event. Then, she took a step back, acknowledging she was being invited for a reason: people acknowledged her work, her vision, and her presence, and she was just as worthy of being on stage as anyone else. Now, Arsheen embraces Impostor Syndrome by pushing herself to give the best possible presentations. Today, Arsheen is often being paid to speak at conferences and events. She has come a long way from when she would shy away from smaller opportunities.

Although Arsheen was taking a big risk by foregoing the six-figure salary offers she watched her Duke MBA classmates accepting, she knew she had the drive to propel her entrepreneurial goals forward. Arsheen let her passion for helping communities in countries like India and Pakistan drive her mission, rather than letting a fear of failure take over.

Arsheen brings up an excellent point about entrepreneurs coming in all forms: extroverts, introverts, ambiverts, you name it. As a very extroverted person myself, I found it fascinating to hear about how being an introvert has allowed Arsheen to become a tremendous leader. The truth is, extrovert or not, you must use your best traits to your advantage, instead of focusing upon your limitations.

Arsheen is continuing to transform the world of clean water and energy, and is paving the way for women pursuing start-ups focused in areas of science.

KEY TAKEAWAYS:
- You don't have to be extremely extroverted to become a successful entrepreneur. Entrepreneurs come in all forms, and can have vastly different personalities.
- It is okay to admit when you have done something wrong. It is incredibly important for successful people to be humble.
- Build your village. Maintain a group of people who support you in all of your endeavors. This group will be there for you through the highs and lows, and have your back when you need it. Your village can be comprised of family members, friends, colleagues, mentors, sponsors, and anyone in between.

CHAPTER 9

THE REVOLUTION AGAINST E-WASTE

———

Imagine you are standing over a bridge with beautiful, crystal clear water beneath you. Someone hands you a laptop and tells you to drop it into the water. Slowly, you see it fall to its tragic death. After you throw the laptop into the water, the person hands you a new one. Then a new one. Then a new one. Now imagine you are standing with eight hundred people. Each of you is handed a laptop. Now you all throw the laptops into the water at the same time. But it does not stop there. All eight hundred people are handed a new laptop to throw into the water each second. There is absolute chaos. Soon enough, the crystal-clear water turns into a pool of grey laptops floating everywhere. Believe it or not, this chaos is the chaos occurring in our world each day.

We generate nearly forty million tons of electronic waste each year.[155] This is equivalent to throwing away eight hundred

---

155 "Electronic Revolution=E-Waste," The World Counts, accessed May 15, 2020.

laptops each second. Electronic waste comprises 70 percent of overall toxic waste, and only 12.5 percent of electronic waste is actually recycled.[156]

These statistics are shocking and, quite frankly, horrifying. Looking back, I received my first ever iPhone when I was in seventh grade. Since then, I have replaced my phone at least every two years, as Apple constantly offers fascinating new updates, styles, and features. When I get a new iPhone, I throw away my old device, which is defunct at this point, into the trash, and I honestly don't think twice about where it may end up. The idea of using an iPhone for a few years, then throwing it out when something "bigger and better" comes out has become completely normalized.

The ugly truth is when people throw their electronics out, waste manifests. Then, the electronic waste enters landfills. Once the waste enters these landfills, it continues to pollute the water, land, and air we swim in, roam on, and breathe in.

In a world where electronic waste remains a pressing issue, Megan O'Connor is providing viable solutions. Megan O'Connor, CEO of Nth Cycle and *Forbes* 30 Under 30 winner in the energy sector, offered me valuable insight about her mission and how she is changing the recycling process of the electronics industry.

---

156 Ibid.

MEGAN'S PATHWAY TO FOUNDING NTH CYCLE:

Megan's pathway to founding a start-up in the energy sector began in college. While attending Union College, Megan became involved with an environmental chemistry lab.

"I loved how I could work in science, something I really enjoyed, while also helping the environment," says Megan.

Combining her interest in science with the environment, Megan decided to pursue a PhD from Duke University in environmental engineering. While in the PhD program at Duke, she began to work on research that now serves a fundamental part of her company. Megan's research at Duke involved figuring out how we could recycle electronics more efficiently.

While in the PhD program, Megan appreciated the interdisciplinary nature of students around her. In an interview with Duke's Civil and Environmental Engineering Department, Megan spoke about how the diversity of students around her made her experience in the PhD program phenomenal.

"You can find people with backgrounds in biology, engineering, chemistry, material science, and more. I come from a chemistry background, so I really struggled with some of the engineering classes in the beginning. Having diverse groups of people to learn from was really helpful in getting me where I am today," says Megan.[157] Through having classes

---

157 Deepti Agnihotri, "Alumni Profile: Megan O'Connor," Duke Civil & Environmental Engineering, April 25, 2018.

with people specializing in many different subjects, Megan had exposure to people pursuing a multitude of tracks.

While pursuing a PhD, Megan did something very atypical; after two years of graduate work, she switched into a completely different project, one that focused on electrochemical recycling. This was a very risky move, but she followed her intuition.

"In the third year of my PhD, I decided I wanted to switch what I was working on entirely. I approached my now cofounder who had developed the original technology behind an electrochemical recycling prototype, and I asked if I could work on the technology for the metals recycling application. Once we had a materials contract with a large manufacturer and really good results recovering their materials, we realized this technology really worked," says Megan.

Seeing the success from the new project provided Megan with the encouragement and motivation to pursue this venture extensively. Despite facing initial concern from her advisor, Desirée Plata, Megan continued to pursue the new project. Desirée did not know if Megan could complete her prototype in the five-year PhD frame, so Megan had to work extra hard to prove herself.

"After working on the technology for three years and many failed attempts, I finally got the prototype to work at the last minute, or within the last six months of my dissertation," says Megan. Instead of allowing herself to give up at any moment, Megan continued to persevere and kept her mission in mind.

After graduating from the PhD program, Megan decided she wanted to continue scaling the electrochemical recycling device and commercialize the unit. After discussing the costs and benefits of launching a start-up with Desirée, Megan decided to pursue the start-up route full force. She applied to different incubators and start-up accelerators, and was soon accepted into Innovation Crossroads.

Innovation Crossroads is a platform providing energy entrepreneurs with early-stage capital, mentorship, and laboratory technology so they can scale their products to commercial levels.[158] With mentorship and support from this program, Megan had an amazing platform to launch her start-up, Nth Cycle.

Since the start of Megan's involvement with Innovation Crossroads, her journey with Nth Cycle has taken off; she is now only three years away from commercialization. Nth Cycle's focus on end-of-life recycling for products brings new, innovative technologies into the clean energy space. Through using carbon nanotube filters to recycle metals from discarded batteries, Megan believes it will become cheaper and more energy efficient for electronics makers to buy recycled metals in the future.[159]

HOW MEGAN HAS OVERCOME CHALLENGES IN THE ENERGY START-UP SPACE:
Throughout Megan's pathway with Nth Cycle, she has faced many challenges along the way. From switching her research

158 "Innovations Crossroads," LinkedIn, accessed May 15, 2020.
159 "About Nth Cycle," Nth Cycle, accessed May 15, 2020.

pathway in the middle of her PhD program, to seeking out ways to fund Nth Cycle, to determining if she needed to pursue an MBA or not, she has faced many hard choices.

I asked Megan about her personal challenges, and how she worked to overcome them.

"I was only twenty-seven when I was considering launching Nth Cycle, and I knew it could go in a lot of different directions. Desirée and I made a pros and cons list, talking about different things like having access to retirement funds or health insurance to see if launching the start-up was worth it. After discussing everything with me, Desirée told me now was the time to launch a new venture. She gave me the motivation to go forward," says Megan.

Because Desirée went through all of the pros and cons with Megan directly, she helped her see the full picture of what it would be like entering the start-up world.

In addition to sharing the importance of having a strong mentor like Desirée, Megan also discussed how she faced great uncertainty launching a start-up without an MBA, or any kind of business experience.

"I applied to MBA programs after receiving my PhD but decided I did not want to go through anymore schooling. While launching Nth Cycle, I was worried my lack of business experience would work against me. Soon enough, I realized after hearing from other entrepreneurs you could learn the same type of skills you would learn from an MBA program through seeking out advice from other people," says Megan.

Megan realized that to learn important concepts of running a business, she had to leverage her entire network. Through maintaining honesty and learning from people she could benefit from, Megan gained more tools to build the platform of Nth Cycle. She obtained meaningful advice from people she networked with, people she went to school with, and her connections at Innovation Crossroads.

"I have learned that most times when startups fail, it is because entrepreneurs pretend like they know everything. It is so important in entrepreneurship to be open and honest with what you know so you can ask the right questions. While working on the business side of Nth Cycle, an MBA could have helped, but it was not absolutely needed. Finding people who could help and mentor me was what mattered the most. Be honest with what you don't know," says Megan.

Following the premise to "be honest with what you don't know," Megan and her co-founders hired a team of people to help them with different facets of the engineering process, and on the technology side. Nth Cycle is now comprised of a team of six people who are very passionate about the mission Megan established.

WHY MEGAN'S PATH IS SO IMPORTANT:

Megan's pathway with Nth Cycle is important because it highlights how mentorship, honesty, and following what you're passionate about can transform your career path. Similar to my conversation with Arsheen, Megan highlights how you must be very interested in what you are pursuing in the start-up world, as you will dedicate an enormous amount of your time to your mission. When I asked Megan for any advice she could provide young women entering the workforce, she emphasized the establishment of networks.

"I had no idea the entrepreneurial path I took even existed, which is why it is so important for women to reach out to as many people as they can in their networks while they are following their career paths. If you're an undergraduate student, use all of the resources available to you; even if older people are not following the same path as you, hearing from their experiences can be incredibly valuable," says Megan.

Megan also highlights how unconventionality can be a key element of success. Rather than following the traditional route of pursuing an MBA before launching a business venture, Megan decided to learn about the business world through networking.

According to Ron Conway, a venture capitalist known as one of Silicon Valley's "Super Angels," "You don't need a business plan. You don't need to have an MBA. All you need is a great idea. Anything is possible and you can accomplish it."[160] In accordance with Ron's ideas, a study conducted by Verdad Research sought to determine if a CEO with an MBA produced a more successful company than a CEO without MBA experience. According to the findings of the study, "MBA programs simply do not produce CEOs who are better at running companies, if performance is measured by stock

---

160 Thomas Oppong, "49 Ways to Become a Better Entrepreneur," LinkedIn, October 30, 2018.

price return."[161] Additionally, on *Fortune*'s "Most Power-ful Women in Business" list, in recent years roughly only one-third of the women on the list received their MBAs.[162] These statistics show that receiving an MBA can certainly be beneficial for female founders and businesswomen, but it is absolutely not necessary. Instead of pursuing a traditional route to understand business concepts, Megan connected with any person she could to gain new insight.

Megan also emphasized the importance of having "cham-pions."

"Keep finding the champions in your life; if you have the determination and grit you can achieve amazing things," says Megan.

If you are able to find someone who believes in you and sup-ports your mission, you have found someone who will likely be there for support and help in times of need. Women can become even more powerful in the workplace if they use their champions to their advantage. Megan used her mentor, Desirée, as an example of one of her champions.

Megan's positive experience with Desirée has inspired her to become an advocate for young women in STEM, and to encourage all entrepreneurs to look for mentors who can support their pathways.

---

161 Dan Rasmussen & Haonan Li, "The MBA Myth and the Cult of the CEO," *Institutional Investor*, February 27, 2019.

162 Seb Murray, "Women Business Leaders Do It Better Without MBAs – Fortune," *BusinessBecause*, September 22, 2014.

HOW MEGAN O'CONNOR OWNS HER IMPOSTOR:

While discussing advice for young women entering the work-force, Megan mentioned that she suffered from Impostor Syndrome but learned how to overcome it.

"I struggled with Impostor Syndrome. With no MBA, busi-ness background, or experience with entrepreneurship, I had to find a lot of people who could help me while launching my startup on the business side of things," says Megan.

Although Megan did not have all of the "checkbox items" some other entrepreneurs have, (like an MBA or business background), she chose to exit her comfort zone and ask for help, rather than face defeat.

Many women suffering from Impostor Syndrome do not like asking for help, as they think it makes them appear weaker, or less competent. Think back to "The Soloist."[163] Allegra, "The Soloist," did not want to ask her resident advisor for help inserting the IV into the fake patient because she thought asking for help would be embarrassing.

Instead of following the principles of "The Soloist,"[164] Megan developed the mindset that you have to accept what you don't know because nobody knows everything. Megan makes it clear that you can't learn and grow until you acknowledge what you don't know.

---

163 Valerie Young, *The Secret Thoughts of Successful Women: Why Capable People Suffer from the Impostor Syndrome and How to Thrive in Spite of It*, (New York: Crown Business, 2011).

164 Ibid.

According to Charlie Munger, the vice chairman of Berkshire Hathaway, which is the conglomerate controlled by Warren Buffett (a.k.a. a source of a lot of money), "Acknowledging what you don't know is the dawning of wisdom."[165] Think about it this way: would you rather work with option a) someone who constantly asks questions about what they don't know, or option b) someone who fakes what they do know? Although it may take "option a" a little bit longer to reach the end goal, they have demonstrated a trait that truly cannot be matched: the desire to learn and grow. The person who learns and grows will almost always surpass what is expected of them and grow as an innovator. Throughout my educational career, I have sought to embrace the traits of "option a," and although I have always been the student who raises my hand or asks questions more than most, I am constantly striving to grow intellectually.

Through acknowledging what she does not know, Megan has formed strong connections with other colleagues and mentors, and serves as a phenomenal mentor herself. Women mentors in STEM are more important now than ever, as the representation of women in STEM fields continues to increase. With strong leaders like Megan offering advice and support to younger women, more women will continue to make progress in STEM.

As Nth Cycle continues to commercialize its technology, Megan continues to highlight strength, resilience, and passion. Megan truly embodies what it means to overcome

---

165 "What You Know?" Investment Masters Class, accessed May 20, 2020.

challenges, self-doubt, and uncertainties, and she continues to accomplish great feats in her journey as a woman in STEM.

KEY TAKEAWAYS:
- Never be afraid to ask for help, or acknowledge what you don't know. Asking for help and seeking out advice helps you become smarter, and build connections.
- If you have to shift a project you're working on, or change the entire trajectory of your path because of obstacles you face, it is okay. It is inevitable you will face challenges and obstacles in your career path, and you have to adapt to them.
- Find people who can serve as your "champions." Your champions will stand by you throughout the highs and lows of your career.
- You don't need a degree in business, or an MBA, to launch a venture. The most impactful tools to excel in the business world can come from your personal experiences and connections.

CHAPTER 10

CHANGING THE WAY AMERICA PAYS FOR COLLEGE

———

Today is the day—you finally have your chance to pitch your game-changing idea to some of the most renowned investors of the entire world: the sharks of *Shark Tank*.[166]

You walk through the deep chamber of the LA studio, and the large, majestic doors open as slowly as a tortoise from *The Tortoise and the Hare*. You have about two minutes to make a lasting impression before the people sitting in the chairs determine the fate of your company. Mark Cuban jots down notes in his notebook, Lori Greiner keeps smiling and nodding (but you can't tell what she's really thinking), and Kevin O'Leary hasn't moved a muscle since you stepped foot into the room. Robert Herjavec looks like he's about to yawn, and

---

166 *Shark Tank,* Season 4 episode 1, "Episode 401," directed by Mark Burnett, aired September 4, 2012, on ABC.

Daymond John keeps looking at his Rolex and new Cartier ring. Last but not least, you can't get over how much Barbara Corcoran looks like Ellen DeGeneres. Do you tell her this? Absolutely not. Although many of the investor fights and drama portrayed on camera is glamorized for reality TV viewers, the *Shark Tank* process is very similar to what it's actually like when young start-up founders try to obtain funding.[167] It is cut-throat, nerve-wrecking, and determined by an overall male audience.

In 2017, *Fast Company and Inc.* conducted a survey of 279 women entrepreneurs and found 62 percent experienced bias during the fundraising process.[168] This survey also asked for feedback about their fundraising experiences, and what it was like pitching their ideas. In the feedback section, one entrepreneur recounted how she was basically told she was too female, and even too blonde. Another spoke about how the funding process felt like speed dating where male investors were making snap judgments, and another was told she would serve as a better media spokesperson than a female CEO.[169]

Female start-up founders face a multitude of challenges and obstacles every step of the way: before launch, during launch, and even after launch. In the overall start-up sphere, they are very underrepresented. But, in the educational technology world, commonly known as ed-tech, female founders are paving the way for greater female representation in the

---

167 Ibid.

168 Pavithra Mohan, "This is what women endure when trying to raise capital." *Fast Company*, September 18, 2018.

169 Ibid.

overarching male start-up world. According to *Fast Company*, 30 percent of ed-tech start-ups include a woman on their founding teams.[170] This value represents nearly twice the percentage of ventures started by women across other technology sectors.[171]

As females in the ed-tech world continue to build traction and overcome obstacles they face as entrepreneurs, they set the precedence for other women to pursue ed-tech venture ideas. As record-hitting venture capital activity takes place for ed-tech, ed-tech incubators, networks, and support groups are rising. In the overall world of entrepreneurship, women in ed-tech are transforming what it means to be a female entrepreneur.[172]

I had the unique opportunity to learn from Charlie Javice, the CEO of Frank, a start-up aimed at making the college admissions process more accessible. I was able to hear further about her experiences in the world of education technology, and how she is writing her story as an entrepreneurial woman in education.

---

170 Jessica Haselton, "Investing in Women-Led Edtech Startups Is More Than a Matter of Equity. It's Also Good Business," *EdSurge*, February 12, 2020.

171 Ibid.

172 Tony Wan, "Is Education Technology Where Women Are Starting to Buck the Tech World's Sexist Trends?" *Fast Company*, April 4, 2015.

FRANK—THE START-UP REVOLUTIONIZING THE COLLEGE FINANCIAL AID PROCESS:

If you were to walk into a room of five hundred randomly selected high school seniors on April 1, the day most universities' regular decisions come out, you would experience a wave of excitement, devastation, and uncertainty all at the same time.

Before opening my early decision answer from Duke, I experienced a million emotions. For the entire week preceding the decision, I checked the portal countless times—even though I knew the site would say the same thing: "Please wait until official decisions come out at 9 p.m. on December 16th." I got less than three hours of sleep the entire week, and even forced myself to do the same ritual every morning before going to school: doing a dance routine I learned in third grade to a Soulja Boy song I swore gave me good luck. I know what you're thinking…my parents thought it was weird too. I prayed and prayed the admissions process would work in my favor, and that I wouldn't end up heartbroken because I knew how much of a crapshoot the process can be. Spoiler alert: if you haven't figured out by now where I attend school—Duke luckily said yes.

The college admissions process can be an emotional roller coaster, and there are so many questions that remain unanswered once it is over. According to a *USA TODAY*/Suffolk University Poll of one thousand registered voters conducted between March 13 and 17, less than 20 percent of Americans think the college admissions process is generally fair.[173]

---

173 Abigail Hess, "Fewer than 1 in 5 Americans think the college admissions process is fair," *CNBC*, March 20, 2019.

As grueling as the admissions process can be, the process of obtaining financial aid is even more difficult. The FAFSA form is currently ranked as the "most complex and convoluted [of] higher [education] forms."[174] Thanks to the complexities of the Free Application for Federal Student Aid form (FAFSA), billions of dollars are not allocated to students who desperately need these funds.[175] Cluttered with complicated phrases and perplexing terms, the FAFSA form discourages many students from applying to financial aid as they do not have the resources to navigate this complex document. Unfortunately, one of the populations most impacted is low-income students.

Charlie Javice, a young entrepreneur from New York, is on a mission to solve this issue. In 2016, Charlie began Frank with the goal of helping all individuals receive the financial aid they deserve. Frank has helped over 350,000 students access financial aid resources and gain access to over seven billion dollars in education funds.[176]

Charlie expressed that one of the most important aspects of beginning a start-up is to remain true to your values and mission.

"In terms of values of the company itself, I guess they almost emulate sort of my personality: being really unfiltered, having

174 Andy Johnston, "One surprising barrier to college success: Dense higher education lingo," *Heching Report.* June 14, 2019.

175 Kim Cook, Kristin Hultquist, Bridget Terry Long and Judith Scott-Clayton, "FAFSA: Ask any college student. The federal student aid application is needlessly complex," *USA Today,* December 9, 2019.

176 "How it Works," Frank, accessed May 25, 2020.

really big opinions, and not being afraid to voice them," says Charlie in an interview with *Popsugar*.[177] Charlie's path in starting Frank exemplifies a key principle of entrepreneurship which is oftentimes overlooked: finding a place where value can be created, and developing a solution.

FINDING A POINT OF VALUE CREATION:

Growing up, Charlie was constantly supported by her parents who encouraged her to chase her dreams.

"I grew up in a household where I was told you work toward something you're passionate about, and if you are successful, you not only do well financially, you can do good in the world," says Charlie.[178]

Charlie immediately took a strong interest in social impact and empowering the lives of others. While observing the world around her, Charlie began to understand why many believe student loans become a business for the government. When students have to pay back abnormally high loans, students face greater and greater holes of debt. After reading and researching the topic, Charlie discovered that in reality, it isn't just the students who are losing money.

"The government is profiting from student loans, but they're really losing billions of dollars a year because people aren't

---

177 Chelsea Adelaine Hassler, "How a 25-Year-Old Woman Is Rebuilding the College Financial Aid Process, 1 Student at a Time," *Pop Sugar*, January 22, 2018.

178 Ibid.

paying it back. It's one of the worst 'success' programs ever," says Charlie.[179]

In 2018, a tweet by Matt Lane exposed one of the many horror stories tied to the student debt crisis. In his tweet, he stated, "I graduated from law school 6 years ago with $250,000 of student loan debt. But after years of hard work and tens of thousands of dollars of payments, I can officially say that I now owe $315,000. Hooray!" Matt is just one example of the thousands of students forced to carry university debt throughout their lifetime, as it continues to build.[180]

In addition to understanding the student debt crisis, through studying education and working in inner city schools, Charlie began to realize how important education was in promoting social equity.

"While volunteering with inner city kids in Philadelphia, I learned so many of them don't view college as a real option, and some even expect to be in prison before they have the chance to graduate from high school," says Charlie in an interview with InHerSight.[181]

When there are so many uncertainties surrounding access to education, students cannot reach the success they deserve. Education is a gateway to success in modern day times. When the college entry process itself is more difficult than it needs

---

179 Ibid.
180 Ilona Baliunaite, "30 Alarming Posts About How the Student Debt System Affects People's Lives and It's Terrible," *Bored Panda.*
181 Cara Hutto, "Meet the Woman Making Quality Education Affordable for All," *Women to Know (blog), In Her Sight*, September 22, 2018.

to be, class differences and inequalities persist. Access to financial aid and understanding its long-term effects is clearly one of the greatest issues incoming college students face.

"In education, there is no way to understand what you are purchasing. It's one of the largest investments most people will make in their entire lives, yet there's no information on how best to pay back the loan you just took out," says Charlie in an interview with Bumble.[182] Due to the circumstances outlined, many high schoolers face having to determine if the hefty price tag for college is even worth it in the long term.

When Charlie graduated from college, she realized her breadth of opportunity, and how it was granted to her from birth.

"It's really an insane kind of light-bulb moment when you realize how lucky you are just to be given that opportunity to do something you love without fear versus being one of the millions of people that kind of have shackles and can't make those kinds of decisions because of student debt—because you're basically working for the government for the rest of your life," says Charlie.[183]

At that moment, Charlie recognized where she could create value: ensuring all individuals had the opportunity to access financial aid. Charlie observed a direct correlation between student debt and students being hindered from reaching their

---

182 "Spotlight: Charlie Javice of Frank," Bumble, Accessed July 5, 2020.

183 Chelsea Adelaine Hassler, "How a 25-Year-Old Woman Is Rebuilding the College Financial Aid Process, 1 Student at a Time," *Pop Sugar*, January 22, 2018.

optimal success. She also observed how difficult the process was in obtaining financial aid to begin with. Through these observations, she discovered that changing the way students interact with the FAFSA form in combination with making financial aid opportunities more transparent could provide a viable solution to the inequities in the financial aid college process.

After discovering where she could make the most impact and upon receiving the monetary funds she needed to move forward, Charlie established a multifaceted platform to achieve one of her primary goals of reaching everyone in need during the financial aid process. Frank's website offers a simpler way to fill out FAFSA, a support team to help with scholarships and applications, in addition to a five-thousand-dollar cash advance for students. Through establishing this multifaceted platform, close to half a million students have gained the support they need.

HOW CHALLENGES CAN HELP YOU GROW STRONGER:
Seeking to tackle the prodigious issue of systematic inequities in the financial aid process for colleges, Charlie has inevitably faced many challenges along the way. In her interview with *PopSugar*, Charlie expressed that one of the greatest challenges she has faced in starting Frank has been "understanding that you're meeting everyone's needs without being too wide, so your message gets diluted."[184]

In addition to working to develop a clear, coherent mission while reaching all potential consumers, Charlie has also

---

184 Ibid.

faced challenges with fundraising and obtaining investors. For most traditional technology companies, investors have a decent idea of what the consumer base will be like, and they have experience in working with these consumers. But Frank had an entirely different consumer base, and Charlie had to work twice as hard to portray the challenges her consumer base faces on a day-to-day basis. This included consumers on benefits, consumers from the lowest socioeconomic statuses, and consumers who worried about how they would be able to pay for their college education.[185]

In addition to helping investors understand her consumer base, Charlie had to connect with these investors on a deeper, more emotional level.

"That was the hard part: explaining to those individuals who are lacking [empathy], to show them the value of working with families and getting involved, in depth, to unearth an opportunity to help them," says Charlie.[186]

Through hard work and continuous moral support from a strong network, Charlie helped Frank capture the attention of investors who believed in her mission. According to TechCrunch, Frank closed a $10 million Series A funding round in December 2017, a $5.5 million seed round earlier that year, and recently raised $5 million in an "interim strategic round."[187]

---

185 Ibid.
186 Ibid.
187 Alex Wilhelm, "Frank raises $5M more in its quest to get students max financial aid," *Tech Crunch*, April 13, 2020.

Charlie found people who believed in her and were also passionate about the power of education, and used these connections to drive Frank's mission forward. Despite being a woman seeking funding from investor panels comprised almost entirely of men, she found a way to attract them to her unique, innovative platform through maintaining an authentic voice.

In addition to promoting education for individuals all across the world, Charlie does a phenomenal job at promoting female empowerment and exposing the true realities of entrepreneurship. From consolidating her mission plan to receiving support from investors to building her Frank team, Charlie has faced a multitude of obstacles.

But she continues to recognize these obstacles as part of her learning process, and they push her mission forward. Charlie's final words from her interview with *InHerSight* encourage women to embrace resilience, understanding "things don't always turn out the way you want them to, but [to] keep trying and don't give up."[188]

Charlie's mission has helped thousands of students attend college and pursue higher education, and seeing her company make tangible change in our educational system is truly inspirational. Oftentimes, people become so overwhelmed with how to begin their missions they lose focus and ultimately lose hope. By focusing on a particular area that corresponds with your talents, immense change is possible.

---

188 Cara Hutto, "Meet the Woman Making Quality Education Affordable for All," *Women to Know (blog), In Her Sight*, September 22, 2018.

Throughout my educational career, one of my overarching goals has been to empower women to pursue their passions, no matter how grand. When deciding whether or not to write this book, one of the doubts I had was understanding if I could make a huge impact in the lives of women with just one book. After deep thought, I realized that even if one woman reads my book and feels inspired, I will have achieved my goal. When women exit their comfort zones to pursue their missions, no matter how grand, they are establishing the precedence for future success and change.

WHY CHARLIE'S PATHWAY IS SO IMPORTANT:
Despite facing a multitude of challenges and having to navigate all of the facets of launching a start-up at a very young age, Charlie stayed true to herself, and to her mission.

In the start-up space, it is so easy to doubt yourself early on, or to think you are never doing enough. In the entrepreneurial world, these types of negative thoughts are extremely common, and many women face Impostor Syndrome early on.

Think back to the example of Rachel, "The Superwoman."[189] On top of Rachel's course load in college, she works part-time at an investment bank, she serves as the student body president, she runs an organization for women in business, and she plays on the club field hockey team. When she forgets

---

189 Valerie Young, *The Secret Thoughts of Successful Women: Why Capable People Suffer from the Impostor Syndrome and How to Thrive in Spite of It*, (New York: Crown Business, 2011).

about one of her commitments, she is extremely hard on herself.

Instead of adapting Rachel's mindset, Charlie emphasizes the importance of rest and maintaining a healthy work-life balance. She mentions how she unplugs one day over the weekend so she can relax and recharge. Charlie works very hard during the week, but ensures that she is not over-committing to tasks.

As a college student who is entering the workforce soon, I have learned maintaining balance is imperative for productivity, and in maintaining a positive attitude. One of the best strategies I have implemented is to create a list detailing what needs to be done ASAP, what has to be done at some point in the week, and what can be done in the future. Through writing out exactly what needs to be done that day, it is much easier to make decisions and avoid being overwhelmed. Additionally, it is extremely satisfying to cross an item off of the ASAP checklist.

When I have accomplished the items for the day, I make a point to do something that brings me genuine happiness. In my life, this is watching Netflix in my bed with Doritos. For some, it means going to yoga. For others it means going on a bike ride. Whatever it is, embrace it, and make sure you get enough of it. Once you have completed the tasks for the day, allow yourself to take a mental break.

As Frank becomes more and more successful, Charlie is changing the face of accessibility to education, while also changing the face of women in the start-up world. She is truly showing the world you can leave a major impact upon society, voice your opinion loud and proud, and still have time for daily yoga.

KEY TAKEAWAYS:
- Women in the start-up space face a wide range of obstacles, particularly in the fundraising process. If you are pitching to a panel of investors, sell them on your story and your mission. Come out confidently, just like you would if you were featured on *Shark Tank*. Investors will not always connect to what you're pitching, but if you are confident, you will showcase your strengths as a founder.
- Make sure you pace yourself, and take mental breaks. Maintaining balance is imperative for successful, hard-working women.
- Acknowledge the privileges you have grown up with and use this knowledge to help others who are less privileged. Oftentimes, acknowledging your privilege enables you to determine where you can help create value, ultimately benefiting your community as a whole.

CHAPTER 11

CODING FOR GIRLS
IS ~COOL~

In middle school, the first day of class was one of the most iconic days of the year. Everyone came in wearing new outfits (mine was always a new Abercrombie and Fitch tee shirt, with light-wash jeans and Converse—and yes, the hall was my personal runway). On the first day of eighth grade, my friends and I walked around the track together, talking about our summer experiences, from Greece trips, to sports camps, to volunteer activities, to lifeguard gigs, to everything in between. This included who was now dating according to the most reliable news source in 2013—Google Buzz. Right after I told my friends about the sprints I had to do each morning at field hockey camp, our friend Francesca told us about her summer coding experience.

I was initially confused, but very intrigued. Coding camp? Is coding a sport? Is it something spies use? Dozens of thoughts ran through my head as I tried to listen to every word she said about coding. Francesca told us how one of her older sisters had majored in computer science in college and was starting to teach younger girls how to code at the beginner level.

When I asked her to explain what coding was, she gave me an in-depth explanation of how coding is responsible for websites, games, computer software, and so many other things. As a fourteen-year-old, I was in awe. Coding seemed like a whole new world, and I felt like I had just received top secret knowledge. Following this experience, I decided to register for an engineering course in high school the next year, as this course incorporated a lot of coding.

The reason I shared this story is not so you could hear about my first day of eighth grade. The truth is, this experience in itself is widely indicative of the need for greater computer science educational opportunities for young women. Until I was fourteen years old, I had no idea what coding meant, even though it served a critical role in my everyday activities and actions. Sarah Filman, *Forbes* 30 Under 30 winner in education, has helped revolutionized access to coding.

SARAH FILMAN—THE LEADER WHO MADE CODING FOR GIRLS ~COOL~

Within the overarching realm of educational technology, Sarah Filman not only made computer science in school more accessible, but she made it both fun and exciting for young women and underrepresented minorities.

Sarah is helping solve a problem that has existed in the education system for decades: a lack of female and minority representation in STEM fields. Throughout my early education,

I immediately noticed I was an outlier as one of the only girls interested in STEM fields. I was one of the only girls on the Science Olympiad team at my elementary school, and one of the only girls on the math team in high school.

One day at recess in September of third grade, I distinctly remember asking several of my friends if they wanted to join Science Olympiad with me during a *High School Musical* rendition. Immediately, they started laughing and saying there was no way they would join a club "filled with annoying boys." As soon as I entered college, I realized the initial disparity between men and women in STEM beginning in early education translates to high school, then college, and ultimately the job pipeline. When I entered college and saw that people were choosing to major in computer science, I was shocked. Quite frankly, I didn't even know a computer science major at Duke existed.

According to the Google report titled, "Science Learning: Closing the Gap," women only make up 25 percent of computing professionals, even though they constitute half the workforce.[190] Furthermore, females are less likely to have studied computer science in school than their male counterparts.[191]

According to the Code.org website, women who have exposure to computer science in high school are ten times more likely to study it in college.[192] Code.org is tackling the lack of

---

190 "Computer Science Learning: Closing the Gap: Girls," Google, accessed May 5, 2020.

191 Ibid.

192 "More Data and Talking Points for Advocacy," Code.org, accessed May 6, 2020.

female representation in computer science head on, offering young women the opportunity to study computer science and pursue jobs in coding if they enjoy it.[193]

At Code.org, Sarah Filman held many different roles: from senior product manager, to vice president of curriculum, to vice president of education. I had the unique opportunity to interview Sarah to learn more about her pathway in transforming the education technology world, and what drives her passion in this area.

FROM BRAIN SCIENCE TO COMPUTER SCIENCE— SARAH'S PATHWAY TO CODE.ORG:

While in high school, Sarah immediately took a liking to math and science classes. When she became a student at Brown University, she was set on majoring in neuroscience. After her first intro to neuroscience class, she realized she was just memorizing concepts and forgetting them after being assessed. Then, computer science hit her like a tornado. Sarah described her first computer science course as "the most challenging course she had ever taken."

"I was used to memorizing concepts, but being in the computer science course pushed me to learn concepts in a new way, which was very difficult. When I finally learned the concepts, there was a learning high that was unbelievable. Working so hard was very appealing, and I loved how computer science was a project-based discipline," says Sarah.

---

193 Ibid.

After deciding to major in Computer Science, Sarah became so passionate about this subject area that she sought to incorporate it into her career pathway. Immediately after graduating, she took on a role as a product manager at Microsoft. While working at Microsoft, Sarah realized she thoroughly enjoyed the teaching and learning behind product development.

After a few years, Sarah became the first full-time product manager of Code.org, "a nonprofit dedicated to expanding access to computer science in schools and increasing participation by women and underrepresented youth."[194] At Code.org, 45 percent of students are girls, 50 percent are underrepresented minorities, and 45 percent of the program's US students are in high needs schools.[195] Code.org provides a diverse range of students with computer science lessons they would've never received elsewhere.[196] Additionally, Code.org tackles the gender gap in STEM in a very unique way. Students can code dance parties featuring music by stars like Katy Perry, they can learn about astronomy, and they can even combine their coding knowledge with *Minecraft* games.[197]

As vice president of education at Code.org, Sarah transformed the pipeline of women and underrepresented minorities entering STEM fields, with a focus in making computer science lessons more accessible.

---

194 "About Us," Code.org, accessed May 6, 2020.
195 Ibid.
196 Ibid.
197 Ibid.

PURSUING OPPORTUNITIES FOR GROWTH:

While speaking with Sarah, I found it fascinating how quickly she moved from a large, corporate space to a mission-driven nonprofit: Microsoft to Code.org. According to Sarah, the biggest difference she observed between her roles at Microsoft and Code.org were that "at Code.org, it was easier to wear different hats."

"At Microsoft, when you're a product manager, you have a team of designers, content writers, people who will market, and there are very compartmentalized roles. At Code.org, as a product manager, if we needed to write a video, I was helping write the script and helping the process end to end," says Sarah. At Code.org, Sarah had less structure within her roles, but more leadership opportunities and chances to showcase her skills.

Furthermore, Sarah noticed many cultural differences between Microsoft and Code.org.

"At Microsoft, I worked with extremely talented individuals who were excited by challenging problems, but at Code.org, my coworkers had an intense passion for students and teachers which was far beyond what I experienced at Microsoft. At a mission-driven nonprofit, it was hard to close off the laptop and go home; it felt like there were higher stakes," says Sarah.

Through her accounts, it became clear that having different types of work experiences can help you grow as a leader, and further understand where your strengths lie. After working at a large corporation for a few years, Sarah understood she enjoyed the education component behind the technology field. So, when offered the opportunity to work at Code.org, a nonprofit focused on education, she considered this as an immense opportunity for growth.

BUILDING CONFIDENCE, CONNECTIONS, AND NETWORKS:

In her shift from for profit to nonprofit companies, Sarah discovered that making in-person connections and building your network can transform your entire career.

"You'll be more effective if you build relationships and talk to people in person; people want to know what you think," says Sarah. Sarah's advice holds true when drawing comparisons to the overall work sphere. According to an article by *Review42*, "a business meeting in person can help you close 40 percent of deals."[198] To reiterate a point I brought up previously, "85 percent of positions are filled by networking."[199]

Although we live in a world continuously shifting with technology, maintaining face-to-face communication is incredibly important. When you are speaking with a client, a businessperson, a colleague, or anyone you come in contact with at work, you are able to sense their emotions, and develop a deeper connection with them. As silly as it may sound, something as simple as a handshake or eye contact can land people jobs and make a lasting impact on new relationships.

---

198 Christina Vukova, "73+ Surprising Networking Statistics to Boost Your Career," *Review42*, February 20, 2020.
199 Ibid.

According to Christine Comaford-Lynch, a female entrepreneur who has successfully founded five different companies including Artemis Ventures, "Networking is marketing. Marketing yourself, marketing your uniqueness, marketing what you stand for."[200] This means that when you network, you have the opportunity to present yourself, and create an impression on others.

Sarah expressed that after ten years in the workforce, she is just now understanding what it means to network effectively. She highlighted that networking should not just be about building up your own career, it should also be tied to how you can help others.

"I started to adapt the mentality that meetings and conversations were not just tied to getting information or help for myself. I wanted to go into them and see how I could help someone else," says Sarah.

Through maintaining this mindset, Sarah realized that even if conversations don't provide an immediate benefit, they can help you unexpectedly in the future.

VALUE-BASED PRINCIPLES ARE THE KEY TO DETERMINING PERSONAL SUCCESS:

When I asked Sarah what she does to maintain a successful mindset, she prefaced her response by saying people should first figure out their own definition of success. She reaffirmed the notion that in current times, we are surrounded by so

200 "Quotes about Recognizing Your Network," *Ellevate.*

many that people think they have the formulaic answer to success.

"We get lots of messages about what success should look like and what your title should be, but it is all up to you," says Sarah. The definition of success for some means having a house and a car, while for others it means having a leadership position in a well-known society, or starting your own freelance business, or helping others through volunteering. The possibilities are endless.

Sarah stayed true to her personal perception of success by reflecting back on potential jobs or opportunities, and asking herself, "Why that?"

"When you are willing to do this type of reflection, asking yourself why you want to pursue a certain opportunity, it can lead to fascinating identifications," says Sarah.

Sarah provides meaningful advice about determining your own definition of success through creating a values list. To help herself in determining her own pathway to success, she makes a list of her top five to eight values she wants to live her life by on a regular basis. Through keeping these values in her head at all times, she is more likely to pursue different opportunities that correspond with these values.

Through Sarah's values assessment, it becomes apparent where you must focus your time and energy in the job search process. For example, if you highly value passion, but you do not think the job you are looking at or applying to can bring this into your life, it is probably a good idea to search for a new role. If something you prioritize is financial security, then it is probably a good idea to search for roles based on salary.

Sarah has widely adapted the values assessment into her own life, as she has worked at places that have helped her improve her confidence, give back to the community, and grow intellectually. She is now exploring organizations, projects, and partnerships where she can work at the intersection of improv, leadership development, and social justice. Sarah believes the "principles of improv comedy and spirit of play can be transformational for personal development, professional development, and team collaboration."

Sarah truly exemplifies the multifacetedness available through different career shifts, and she displays how your specific job role is not indicative of success in life; your success in life stems from your mindset and whether or not you are following your core values.

WHY SARAH'S PATH IS SO IMPORTANT:

Throughout Sarah's career, she stresses the importance of maintaining confidence, building connections, and being true to yourself. This has landed her onto the *Forbes* 30 Under 30 list. However, she is also incredibly honest about how she was not always as confident as she is today.

Sarah suffered from Impostor Syndrome when she wouldn't raise her hand or answer a question unless she was 100 percent sure of the answer. Women in the workplace suffering from Impostor Syndrome oftentimes do not speak up for themselves unless they are completely sure their answer or approach is correct.

Again, think back to the story of Hanna, "The Expert."[201] Hanna did not apply for a grant providing clean water solutions because she did not think her background checked everything on the requirements list.

In the same manner that Hanna did not apply for the grant because she did not think her experience was worthy enough, Sarah would not raise her hand at the start of her career because she was not sure if her answer was correct. To overcome this internal battle, Sarah began to take risks, acknowledge her answer was important, and raise her hand, even if she wasn't sure the answer was correct.

According to Sarah, "the person who has gotten most in my way has been myself." She recounted how for the first four years of her career, her confidence stood in the way of her progress.

Sarah also recounted how she primarily used email in the earlier phases of her career, and did not go out of her way for in-person networking. Why was this? She was an introvert, and she did not think in-person meetings were always necessary. After realizing how these initial thoughts held her back, Sarah decided to adopt a new mentality in the workplace.

---

201 Valerie Young, *The Secret Thoughts of Successful Women: Why Capable People Suffer from the Impostor Syndrome and How to Thrive in Spite of It*, (New York: Crown Business, 2011).

Through building relationships with mentors, Sarah began to realize that so many people wanted to hear her thoughts, and her opinion was incredibly valuable.

Adapting this mindset ultimately helped Sarah make an enormous impact for women and underrepresented minorities in STEM by ensuring this arena was more inclusive. Sarah is a leading woman in education, and she continues to drive change in each new area she tackles.

KEY TAKEAWAYS:
- Define your OWN version of success. What are your goals tied to? What do you want to accomplish in life? What does success mean to you?
- Conduct a values assessment regularly. Determine your work needs and motivations, and see if what you're doing falls in accordance with these values.
- Raise your hand even if you don't know the answer to something. This will help you build confidence and make connections.
- Job shifts between different types of companies can transform your leadership skills, and help you determine where you can provide the most value.

CHAPTER 12

REPORTING FROM A REVOLUTION

———

It is the summer of 2013. Four radical jihadists and a blonde American reporter sit down for dinner a few miles from a battlefield in Syria. At this dinner, the group breaks bread and converses about a wide range of topics, from their schooling experiences, to family, to even their love life.[202]

The reporter suddenly spills her tea. One of them quickly remarks, "You wouldn't be so scared if you had Allah…!"[203]

One of the jihadists, Ayman, begins to talk about how he learned English for the first time. "I first started learning English from American cartoons, but when I got older, I really liked *Boy Meets World*. Do you know it?"[204]

———

202 Anna Therese Day, "Dining with Al Qaeda," *The Daily Beast*, July 11, 2017.
203 Ibid.
204 Ibid.

After talking about schooling experiences and hopes for a future with beautiful wives, the men discuss with the reporter their aspirations to reach "Paradise" as suicide bombers. The men talk about how competitive it is to be selected for suicide bomb missions, and how it is their greatest dream to be chosen. All four of the radical jihadists are members of the terrorist group known as ISIS, and they discuss their lives as ISIS members in great depth.[205]

At the end of the dinner, the young man named Faraz tells the reporter, "Tell America: we will fight you where ever you kill more Muslims. We are ready when you are."[206]

This story is a rendition from "Dining with Al Qaeda," Anna Therese Day's experience as a twenty-five-year-old woman sitting down for dinner with four members of ISIS. In "Dining with Al Qaeda," Anna recounts her experience meeting Mohammed, Ayman, Faraz, and Ahmad, four radical jihadists who sought to share their stories with a Western audience.[207]

Anna Therese Day is a revolutionary reporter and filmmaker whose journey has been defined by courage, curiosity, and passion. Her work has been featured across a multitude of platforms including: *CNN*, *Al Jazeera English*, *BBC*, *CBS*, and *Vice Media*, among others.[208] In 2017, Anna was named on the *Forbes* 30 Under 30 list in the media category for her work in advancing the intersection of international politics, social

---

205 Ibid.
206 Ibid.
207 Ibid.
208 "About," Atdlive.com, accessed October 5, 2020.

movements, human rights, technology, and security. Anna has been at the center of revolutions, she has been detained in uprisings, and of course, she has dined with terrorist organizations.

I had the opportunity to speak with Anna and learn about her mission in addition to how she has developed unique opportunities for herself as a young, female journalist.

WOMEN IN JOURNALISM—A CONTINUOUS, UPHILL BATTLE:

To analyze Anna's impact in the journalism community, it is important to take a step back to understand the scope of the industry.

According to the ASNE Diversity Survey, "each year, women comprise more than two-thirds of graduates with degrees in journalism or mass communications, and yet the media industry is just one-third women."[209] So, why does female representation in journalism diminish post-graduation? What drives the disparity between men and women in journalist positions? How can these statistics change? These are all questions that desperately need to be addressed because the percentage of women in journalism has remained stagnant.

According to a study by Scott Reinardy, a professor at the University of Kansas, "the percentage of female journalists

---

209 Catherine York, "Women dominate journalism schools, but newsrooms are still a different story," *Poynter*, September 18, 2017.

more than doubled between 1900 and 1971. But, once it reached 37 percent in 1999, it plateaued."[210] This means the journalism industry was inching toward gender parity and equality, but suddenly stopped. Why is this? Women have reported higher levels of role overload than men, men are more present in the editor roles in charge of hiring and promoting, and of course, the mid-career gap persists as women take on familial roles.[211]

In addition, according to the International Women's Media Foundation, "nearly one-third of early career women journalists consider leaving the profession due to attacks and harassment."[212] On top of gender bias and limited opportunities to advance, an overwhelming number of women in journalism do not feel safe or comfortable in the workplace.[213] This desperately needs to change.

Despite the current arena of journalism, Anna Therese Day has created a name for herself.

ANNA'S JOURNEY IN JOURNALISM:

Anna studied political science at the University of Wisconsin-Madison while the US was at war with Iraq. Because of the political climate of the time, Anna had direct exposure to the world changing before her eyes. Early on, she knew

---

210 Ibid.
211 Ibid.
212 "19 women changing journalism in 2019," International Women's Media Foundation, accessed October 5, 2020.
213 Ibid.

she wanted to capture stories as they unfolded to share what was taking place with the rest of the world.

"Early on in college, I received the advice to learn new languages if I wanted to cover international stories. After receiving this excellent advice from teachers, I sought after opportunities to study abroad in the Middle East," says Anna.

After pursuing a study abroad program in the Middle East in her undergraduate years, she saw firsthand how people were fighting for their freedom. This compelled Anna to pursue a master's degree at Ben-Gurion University of the Negev, focusing upon Arab-Israeli relations and the Israeli-Palestinian conflict. Anna was immediately drawn to the social revolutions taking place in the Middle East at this time and she knew reporting here would fulfill her dreams.

Anna particularly recounted her experience at a protest in Cairo, at the start of the Egyptian revolution in 2011. The revolution centered around young people seeking to overthrow the autocracy of President Hosni Mubarak, who had been in power for nearly thirty years.[214]

"When I heard a revolution might take place in Cairo, I immediately traveled there to see it unfold firsthand. This was one of my first opportunities as a journalist, and I was a young woman walking around with a dinky camera who looked like a tourist. On the very first day of the revolution, the government blocked all of the blogs and social media sites demonstrators were organizing on. When I walked

---

214 "Egypt Revolution: 18 days of people power," *Al Jazeera,* January 25, 2016.

toward Tahrir Square, I could hear the demonstrators loud and proud before I could see them. This was one of the most transformative moments of my career," says Anna.

Eighteen days after the revolution began, President Mubarak announced his resignation, signifying that the people desperately seeking change had won.[215] This demonstration shaped the rest of Anna's career, as she had firsthand exposure to stories of people valiantly fighting for their freedom.

Following the experience in Egypt, Anna continued to report in the Middle East. When the Syrian War began, Anna was already well-sourced with young Arab activists throughout the region, which enabled her to begin her reporting on the conflict there.

"I quickly learned to use my age and gender as an advantage in my career. I was living on the border in cheap hotels in Casablanca-esque, lawless communities, and I met a number of interesting people who were coming to fight in the Syrian War. These people ended up joining groups like Al Qaeda and ISIS, and after meeting them, I established connections so I could interview them and hear their stories," says Anna.

After reporting in the Middle East for several more years, Anna was named a Fulbright fellow, and reported in Madrid. Since then, she has been a regular contributor to the *New York Times,* she co-founded the independent multimedia documentary house Fovrth Studios, and she was a founding board member of the *Frontline Freelance Register.* Anna

---

215 Ibid.

was recently named a recipient of the James Foley World Press Freedom Award for her reporting and press freedom advocacy.

TRAILBLAZING LIKE ANNA:
Anna has been a trailblazer for thousands of women in journalism, and as time passes, she continues to set the precedence for female reporters. I asked Anna what advice she would offer young women starting their careers.

"When you're young, you have to be hungry. No one owes you anything, and you have to make sure you have a very strong work ethic. Even if things don't move fast in your career, you have to constantly find ways to develop on your own," says Anna.

Through her incredible work ethic, Anna gained access to fascinating, new opportunities. She walked the streets of Cairo tirelessly to report about freedom, she learned entire new languages at the age of twenty, and she immersed herself in countless conflicts and revolutions to share stories with others. No one told her she had to do these things, but she knew she had to so she could achieve her goals as a reporter.

Similar to Anna, I have learned that your work ethic can make or break you. Throughout high school, I played field hockey. Before I tried out for the team, I was by far one of the worst players from a technical standpoint. I could barely hit the ball without getting the stick stuck into the ground, and I had to tape game plays onto my stick so I wouldn't forget them.

Every single day before tryouts, I came to training thirty minutes early and stayed thirty minutes after, practicing shots on my own. As the days progressed, I became better and better, slowly learning plays and drills on my own. When tryouts began, my running skills and work ethic helped me earn a spot on the team.

Although reporting in the middle of social revolutions is slightly different than making the roster of a high school sports team, the same lesson applies: if you want to accomplish a feat that seems unattainable, you must be willing to put in the work and drive forward.

One of my favorite Mark Cuban quotes is, "Do the work. Out-work. Out-think. Out-sell your expectations. There are no shortcuts."[216] Anna preaches the same thing, stressing how important it is to exceed expectations of yourself and of others.

WHY ANNA'S STORY IS SO IMPORTANT:
While listening to Anna's story, it was very apparent that she never chased after the "perfect story"; she worked extremely hard, immersed herself in new situations, and was always curious. Oftentimes, women suffering from Impostor Syndrome work extremely hard, but chase after unrealistic ideas of perfection. Think back to the story of Sarah, "The Perfectionist."[217] As a digital media consultant, Sarah worked more

216 Jenna Goudreau, "Mark Cuban Reveals the Best and Worst 'Shark Tank' Pitches and More," *Business Insider*, November 11, 2013.

217 Valerie Young, *The Secret Thoughts of Successful Women: Why Capable People Suffer from the Impostor Syndrome and How to Thrive in Spite of It*, (New York: Crown Business, 2011).

hours than necessary, perfecting presentations, re-reading slides, and obsessing over little details.

Rather than chasing after perfection, Anna focused on how her work was aligning with her mission, practicing self-reflection often. An active way to avoid the feelings tied to "The Perfectionist" competence type is to reflect upon how you perceive perfection, and to applaud yourself for what you have already accomplished. As a female journalist who is trailblazing for young women all across the world, Anna remains focused on what she has brought to the table, and how she can continue to excel.

Women like Anna are changing the world as we know it, proving to young women that they have what it takes to break into journalism. As news writing and reporting continues to evolve, Anna displays how important it is to stay hungry, be proactive, and advocate for change. You don't have to dine with ISIS to rise to the top, but you do have to push yourself, own up to your achievements, and chase after new opportunities like no other.

KEY TAKEAWAYS:

- Immersing yourself in unpredictable situations can transform your whole life. It is very important to exit your comfort zone to explore new opportunities, and to grow as an individual.
- You are never too young to take on a daunting task. Society has instilled the perception within us that the older you get, the wiser you become. This is not always true. If

you're a young person entering an industry, use your age as an advantage.

- No one owes you anything. Remember that. Work extremely hard, and test your limits. This can and will pay off when you are chasing your goals.

CHAPTER 13

CLAPPING WITH TWO HANDS

Have you ever tried to clap with just one hand? Pause for ten seconds and see if you can do it. You may be trying to use your fingers right now for traction, trying to move your wrist around to see if you can hit your palm from an angle, or if you're like me, you've given up.[218]

This is the question Sally Nuamah, award winning professor, filmmaker, and researcher asked her audience at a TEDx Talk held in 2013 at University of Chicago.[219] She asked the audience this question, and then laughed as she saw their unique takes in action.

After seeing what the audience came up with, the general consensus the audience reached was that it is nearly impossible to clap with one hand. Sally then asked the question,

---

218 *TEDx Talks*, "Clapping with One Hand: Sally Nuamah at TEDxUofIChicago," May 3, 2013, video, 11:46.
219 Ibid.

"What is the point of clapping with one hand, if you have two?"[220]

This brought her to the next part of the conversation, where she reflected upon and quoted a famous women's rights activists who asked this question and inspired her to give the TEDx Talk in the first place.

"Trying to develop a nation without including women as part of that process is like telling a person to clap with one hand."[221] In other words, women play instrumental roles in the everyday functions in each nation of the world.

Sally reflected on how there has been "a lot of one-hand clapping" taking place in society, and the solution lies in education.[222] She then dove into a conversation about educational structures of the world, where inequities exist, and how the world can overall do so much better.

Sally Nuamah is a professor at Northwestern University, an award-winning scholar, the author of *How Girls Achieve*, founder of the TWII Foundation Girls Scholarship, and director of the film *HerStory*. She was named on the *Forbes* 30 Under 30 list in education, and was recently presented the prestigious Andrew Carnegie Fellowship award, also known as the Brainy Award.[223]

---

220 Ibid.
221 Ibid.
222 Ibid.
223 "Short Bio," SallyNuamah.com, Accessed October 7, 2020.

While speaking with Sally, I learned about her perspectives on education, and gained great insight into how she is transforming education for women across the globe.

USING PAST EXPERIENCES TO DRIVE YOUR FUTURE GOALS:

Growing up as a black woman in Chicago in the 1990s, Sally immediately acknowledged she was at a disadvantage from others. After her parents fled from Ghana during a military coup, they took on many different jobs as low-income workers. Sally grew up in government subsidized housing close to the Cabrini-Green homes, and she immediately realized income and class disparities.

"I grew up with an eye that people had more than others," says Sally. She noticed this in schools, in the transportation system, and even while walking down the streets of her neighborhood.

As Sally grew up, she immediately recognized education was one of the only factors in her life she possessed full autonomy over. She could not control where she was raised, how much money she had growing up, or her social class, but she could control her education. One day, her mother was in the parking lot of her workplace, and the principal asked where Sally was attending school next.

"When my mom told him my options, he said 'whatever you do, go to the more selective school.' When I heard this story, I realized how crucial your educational experience is in shaping your career and life pathway," says Sally.

After realizing that education was the key factor in helping her improve her life circumstances, Sally was driven to help other underprivileged women in the world improve their lives through education.

Following this realization, Sally went on to produce a documentary, write a book, conduct research on gender and race inequality, and serve as a professor and international advocate for women's rights. Rather than following a defined career pathway, Sally utilized her upbringing and life experiences as her source of inspiration in many different roles.

TACKLING THE FLAWS IN THE EDUCATION SYSTEM HEADFIRST:

As a first-generation Ghanaian American, Sally has overcome a multifaceted set of obstacles to distinguish herself in society.

She has truly defined herself as a powerful force in the education of women through her award-winning film, *HerStory*. This film follows the lives of Ghanaian girls completing their last years at the West African Secondary School. *HerStory* compels viewers to think about education as a powerful tool to help women all over the world break free from poverty.

But Sally does not stop there. On top of emphasizing the importance of education, she also examines what changes are needed in the educational world before it can truly become a safe place where all women can grow. Throughout her studies, she emphasizes that educational systems in place internationally have a long way to go before they can become equitable for both young girls and boys. Sally frequently addresses the high presence of sexual assault and harassment that make many schools unsafe places for young girls.

"If a girl is enrolled in school because of an educate-the-girl-child campaign, but her school is a site of sexual violence, is the fact she attends school enough to call that campaign a policy success? Or if a girl attains good grades in school, perhaps even better than her male classmates, but has been raped in the process, is her education worth the trauma she endured?" says Sally in a *Washington Post* piece.[224]

Here, Sally expands upon her argument that education is necessary; however, she also addresses that in addition to greater representation of girls in schools, there also need to be more policies in place to prevent sexual assault, and to punish sexual assault perpetrators.[225]

In the same *Washington Post* article, Sally references her time in Ghana, where she interviewed a Ghanaian expert who spoke about "STGs—Sexually Transmitted Grades."[226] This term was used "to describe the experience of girls being asked to perform sexual favors in exchange for accurate reporting of their grades."[227] In settings designated for young women to grow socially and intellectually, they were forced to perform sexual acts so that their accomplishments would be noted correctly.

---

224 Sally A. Nuamah, "On the International Day of the Girl, it's a good time to ask: are girls safe in school?" *The Washington Post*, October 11, 2018.
225 Ibid.
226 Ibid.
227 Ibid.

Sally not only revealed this through her documentary, but has also used her voice to then begin the TWII Foundation. The TWII Foundation aims to provide funding for girls seeking to become the first ones in their families to go to college. In addition to promoting the TWII Foundation, Sally released her first book *How Girls Achieve* in 2019. *How Girls Achieve* reflects how education plays an important role in the lives of women, and she describes the types of educational foundations necessary for ensuring equitable education for girls all across the world. Sally follows stories of women in the US, South Africa, and Ghana to highlight how education systems do not truly support women in low, middle, or developed nations.

One of the topics Sally addresses in the book is the development of "feminist schools." When I asked Sally to expand upon what the ideal institution would look like, she tied in her personal life.

"When I think about the ideal educational institution, I think about a school I would want my child to attend. At so many schools, students suffer from high levels of anxiety and depression, and I would not want my child attending an institution that perpetuates these things," says Sally.

Sally expands upon the ideas of what comprises her ideal educational institution in an interview with the *Duke Chronicle*. In this article, she talks about her own observations of different schools in Ghana, including the lack of menstrual care products.[228] She also saw that after high school gradua-

---

228 Stefanie Pousoulides, "Sally Nuamah on how punishment against black girls impacts our democracy," *The Chronicle*, August 8, 2019.

tion, most girls could not attend college because they did not have the financial means to do so.[229] The young women at Ghanaian schools did not have the health, social, educational, or financial support to succeed.

SALLY'S IMPORTANT ADVICE ON ACHIEVING GOALS:

While speaking with Sally about overcoming obstacles and achieving your personal goals, she emphasized the first thing young people should do is have a mission. She highlighted that when young people think about their futures, they are often plagued by false societal expectations.

"It is important for young people to follow the purpose they intend for their lives," says Sally.

In addition, Sally also expressed young people should adapt their mission to the current conditions of the time; she herself did this during the COVID-19 pandemic. In the middle of the pandemic, Sally used her passion for educating others to assist a community organization dedicated to informing people of COVID-19 preventative measures. Through educating communities about COVID-19 preventative measures, she found where she could utilize her strengths to make the most immediate change. Sally also stressed that you need to stay focused on your mission and that you don't have to "do it all" to be considered successful.

Women in the modern-day workplace often suffer from thinking they have to "do it all," and even when they have

---

229 Ibid.

accomplished amazing things, they still have a lot more to do.

In my life as a college student, I have suffered from the need to "do it all" particularly while working on my honors thesis. My thesis tackles the prodigious issue of human trafficking in North Carolina, and I analyzed the practices antihuman trafficking stakeholders follow. While initially starting this thesis, I knew it would be very difficult. Human trafficking is a very important topic, but there are so many questions left unanswered. Rather than trying to tackle every single question, I started small. I researched nonprofits, then coalitions, then legal organizations, slowly understanding how preventative efforts could improve. Instead of allowing myself to be overwhelmed with everything I didn't know, I started focusing on what I did know. With this knowledge, I was able to successfully complete my thesis, and ultimately help the fight against human trafficking in North Carolina.

Now, think back to the story of Rachel, "The Superwoman."[230] Rachel has a part-time internship, she is a full-time student, and she maintains an extensive list of extracurricular activities. She tries to do it all, but if something goes wrong as she tries to balance everything, she is extremely hard on herself.

Sally's advice is that women should not try to do it all, but instead focus on following their own specific mission. This does not entail working strenuously just to say you did or to reaffirm a false sense of confidence.

---

230 Valerie Young, *The Secret Thoughts of Successful Women: Why Capable People Suffer from the Impostor Syndrome and How to Thrive in Spite of It*, (New York: Crown Business, 2011).

It is crucial that young people use their drive, passion, and energy to establish their mission, or goal in life, and go after it. Sally is a revolutionary thinker, and she serves as a tremendous role model for young people all across the globe. She is truly transforming the globe into a place where people are clapping with two hands.

KEY TAKEAWAYS:
- Your mission can take you in many different directions. You may go from writing, to researching, to producing films, to teaching university students. No matter where your journey takes you, use these experiences to discover your mission and pursue your end goals.
- You have the ability to help tackle major, systematic issues in the world. Just because an issue is big in scope, it does not mean you don't have the ability to make a change.

CHAPTER 14

FROM CORPORATE AMERICA TO THE START-UP WORLD

During 2018, drug overdoses led to 67,367 deaths in the United States.[231] Opioids were involved in 46,802 of these deaths.[232] However, addiction is oftentimes not recognized as one of the leading causes of death in the United States. Despite the existence of thousands of in-patient centers and facilities in place to mitigate the effects of addiction, the number of individuals suffering from addiction continues to increase each year.

Why is this? Stephanie Papes, entrepreneur and 2019 recipient of the *Forbes* 30 Under 30 award in health care is revolutionizing the way we look at this question. Stephanie Papes

---

231 Nana Wilson, PhD; Mbabazi Kariisa, PhD; Puja Seth, PhD; Herschel Smith IV, MPH; Nicole L. Davis, PhD, "Drug and Opioid-Involved Overdose Deaths—United States, 2017–2018," CDC, March 20, 2020.

232 Ibid.

is the founder and chief executive officer of Boulder Care, a healthcare start-up expanding patient access to treatment and support services for opiate and other substance use.[233]

I spoke with Stephanie to gain greater insight about her background as an entrepreneur, in addition to her mission behind founding Boulder Care.

HOW A PASSION FOR IMPROVING HEALTH CARE LED STEPHANIE INTO THE START-UP SPACE:

As a young student at Duke University, Stephanie immediately grew passionate for healthcare reform. Her public policy major allowed her to see how healthcare policies and practices inevitably shaped the lives of millions of people across the United States. While interning on Capitol Hill, she saw the development of these healthcare policies firsthand.

"When I interned in DC for a healthcare consulting firm, I loved learning about the healthcare world and major shifts on the horizon. I became so passionate about wanting to make health care more accessible and affordable," says Stephanie.

Stephanie's passion for more accessible and affordable health care stems from the extremely high costs of healthcare treatment in the United States today, and from inequitable access to treatment across socioeconomic classes, races, zip codes, genders, and certain conditions that carry stigma.

---

233 "Stephanie (Papes) Strong," LinkedIn, accessed September 28, 2020.

In a poll conducted by Gallup in December 2019, findings reported a quarter of Americans have had to delay medical treatment of serious illnesses due to high costs.[234] This means at least one out of four people suffering from a life-threatening illness cannot receive treatment on time. Furthermore, the Gallup poll revealed that 34 percent of Americans have had to delay medical treatment for less serious illnesses due to high costs.[235]

In addition, there is evidence that gender bias exists in the healthcare treatment process, particularly in treatments for cardiovascular disease, mental health, and pain. According to Amy M. Miller, PhD, president and CEO of the Society for Women's Health Research, "With society often dismissing women's pain and a relatively brief record of research inclusive of women, it is unsurprising many of the chronic pain conditions for which we do not have direct treatments are more common in or exclusively affect women."[236] Miller highlights how in some situations, women feel their pain levels weren't taken seriously due to dismissive behavior amongst healthcare providers.[237]

Seeking to further expand her passion for improvements in the healthcare system, Stephanie began to work within the Duke University Medical Center. Stephanie worked on a project developing a system-wide roll-out of electronic

---

234 Michael Sainato, "The Americans dying because they can't afford medical care," *The Guardian*, January 7, 2020.

235 Ibid.

236 Thomas Jefferson University Online, "Exploring Gender Bias in Healthcare," *MedCityNews*, September 4, 2019.

237 Ibid.

health records for the first time, spanning 250 facilities. She also worked on a new payment and delivery model design for family clinics, which became Duke's Accountable Care Organization.

"As I worked on different projects at Duke, I quickly began to realize how important technology and services integration was in care delivery," says Stephanie.

Soon enough, the experience from the clinics at Duke translated into Stephanie's career path. After working as an investment banking analyst for two years, Stephanie joined a venture capital firm called Apple Tree Partners. Apple Tree Partners is a firm that focuses specifically on building life science companies.[238] As an associate at this firm, Stephanie had direct exposure to helping companies that were changing the face of health care.

While at Apple Tree Partners, one of the portfolio investments Stephanie had a role in was the investment in a platform of addiction centers.

"While working with this portfolio company, I would hear stories firsthand of people regaining custody over their children after overcoming their opioid addiction, and truly transforming their lives. But, I realized there is a lot of stigma and misinformation about how opioid addiction is treated. For the limited communities who have access to evidence-based treatment, there are not enough programs

---

238 "Approach," Apple Tree Partners, accessed September 30, 2020.

successfully retaining people in a sustainable treatment model," says Stephanie.

Stephanie realized we needed to change the way we talk about addiction. Seeing that people came into addiction centers and were asked to go to pharmacies, counselors, coaches, and clinicians all in different places, she saw an immediate flaw in the addiction treatment system: there was no cohesive place combining all of the facets of addiction treatment together, placing undue burden on the patient.

Combining her background in business with her passion for advocating for others in the healthcare system, Stephanie decided to launch her own start-up called Boulder Care. Boulder Care is an innovative mobile healthcare platform dedicated to providing people recovering from opioid addiction with a care team comprised of a clinician, peer coach, and care advocate all from a singular app.[239]

THE PLATFORM BEHIND BOULDER CARE:
When I asked Stephanie about the platform of Boulder Care, she emphasized that her goal was to help all individuals receive the addiction care and treatment they need and deserve.

In an article Stephanie wrote on *Medium,* she states, "patients are forced to navigate a complicated, often predatory system entirely on their own: contradictory medical advice.

---

239 "About Boulder Care," Boulder Care, accessed September 30, 2020.

Judgmental stares. Rehab facilities promising a 'cure' for $60,000 in cash."[240]

On top of these obstacles, patients seeking treatment must also navigate the process of finding and scheduling appointments with counselors, clinicians, pharmacists, and labs—all entities that do not communicate with each other. In this process, populations or people who do not have the time nor resources to access so many different specialists are inevitably at a disadvantage.[241]

Through providing a universal platform for telemedicine, Stephanie thinks she can fix many of the systematic flaws of the addiction treatment system.

"Sometimes, patients leave the hospital after nearly fatal overdoses with simply a pamphlet," says Stephanie. She highlights how instead of receiving a multifaceted treatment plan to help them return to their everyday lives, many people suffering from overdoses receive bare minimum support.

In addition to seeing how patients experiencing relapses have barely any help in place, Stephanie also acknowledges it is very hard for patients to receive customized care treatments for their journeys.

"While having to juggle counselors, clinicians, and pharmacists, patients oftentimes do not have a customized treatment plan that works specifically for them," says Stephanie.

---

240 Stephanie Papes, "We know how to treat opiate addiction: now we must get care to patients," *Medium*, March 13, 2018.
241 Ibid.

To solve the issue of the lack of customized treatment plans in combination with the lack of a universal treatment platform, Stephanie developed a three-pronged path to wellness for Boulder Care patients. The Boulder Care path to wellness incorporates proven treatment from licensed addiction specialists, a dedicated care team to support participants with "expert medical care, peer recovery coaching, and care coordination," and an easy-to-access digital platform.[242]

Boulder Care's platform has been extremely successful so far, and has expanded its reach to Alaska, Oregon, and Washington. In February 2020, Boulder Care announced $10.5 million in Series A funding, and is continuing to expand.[243]

Stephanie was able to turn her knowledge into an impetus for change. Some of her most memorable experiences working for Boulder include "seeing families reuniting, people go back to things they formerly loved like school, sports, art, and music, transitioning into safer housing, and seeing people's lives change both rapidly and progressively, for the better." She also shared patient testimonials left publicly on Boulder Care's Facebook page:

"All it takes to change your life is a phone call. It changed mine."[244]

---

242 "About Boulder Care," Boulder Care, accessed September 30, 2020.
243 Kyle Coward, "Boulder Care Announces $10.5M in Series A Funding," *Behavioral Health Business*, February 14, 2020.
244 Boulder Care, Facebook.

"Thank you for everything you do, have done and continue to do to make a difference in the lives of those who struggle to make sense of it all. I don't know where I'd be without you!"[245]

These accounts truly exemplify how start-ups do not only shape technology, policies, and ideas, but they can also impact individuals on a personal level.

WHY STEPHANIE'S PATH IS SO IMPORTANT:

Stephanie discovered her pathway through experience, as she found she was passionate about advocating for others in the healthcare system. Learning through experience is one of the many viable ways for female entrepreneurs to discover their passions. With endless opportunities for change in the world, many people become overwhelmed while determining the best approaches to take, and where to even start. This often deters people from pathways of start-ups and entrepreneurship, where uncertainties appear to be omnipresent. With constant concerns surrounding funding, marketing, product development, and strategy, it is very difficult for many to take the leap of faith that leads to innovation in the world.

I experienced this sensation while I was a young, aspiring entrepreneur in high school. When I was in tenth grade, I came up with the idea to launch a baklava ice cream food truck: a unique take on the typical ice cream truck, offering the Greek dessert baklava as a topping. After seeing this concept become rapidly successful at the Greek festival at my church each year, I knew it could become a hit if it was

---

245 Ibid.

commercialized and set in motion. While generating a business plan for the food truck, I did not realize how many components were behind it. I had to come up with funding, target locations, employees, and food suppliers. Because I was balancing eight classes, an extensive list of extracurriculars, and a sport, I decided it was not the right time. (Trust me, the baklava truck will have its moment to shine some day.)

When I asked Stephanie what advice she would give young, entrepreneurial women, she provided very insightful information.

"It is so important you do not second-guess your ability to have a brilliant idea and to actually make it happen," says Stephanie.

Stephanie also recounted it is incredibly important to bring positive people onto your mission who have experience in the field you're interested in, whether they will serve as mentors, coworkers, or people to engage in conversation with. The most helpful people have been those who offer critical, honest feedback and aren't afraid to challenge your assumptions, but come from a place of genuine belief in your vision and leadership, shared goals of success, and trust in your ability to ultimately make the best decisions.

As the founder and chief executive officer of Boulder, Stephanie manages a large team where she is exposed to people of many different ages, backgrounds, and experiences. Through aligning her team toward the common goal of providing easy, accessible addiction treatment, Stephanie and her team members combine their individual strengths to create impact in the healthcare world. When you associate with negative energy and people who make you question your ability to succeed, you will express the same negative energy, and you are ultimately more likely to fall victim to Impostor Syndrome.

People hit especially hard from Impostor Syndrome during the start-up process may fall under the competence type known as "The Soloist."[246] Think back to the story of Allegra. When Allegra was in medical school, she did not ask the resident advisor for help while trying to insert the IV because she thought it would make her look incompetent. After she asked the resident assistant for help, she realized if she had asked him sooner, she would've been able to insert the IV in ten seconds.

Rather than fearing she would appear less competent when asking for help, Stephanie sought help from mentors and people with experience to successfully carry out her platform for Boulder Care. Now, Stephanie champions her web of support and people who she can ask questions to, and this is one of the reasons she has been able to run her venture successfully.

Additionally, because everyone on Stephanie's team believes in her mission, they are able to successfully question the old models of health care that are inevitably excluding populations from receiving support. Through utilizing a unified approach behind solving an issue, Stephanie's platform is constantly expanding.

---

246 Valerie Young, *The Secret Thoughts of Successful Women: Why Capable People Suffer from the Impostor Syndrome and How to Thrive in Spite of It*, (New York: Crown Business, 2011).

Although Impostor Syndrome is an internal battle, it is largely attributed to the people you surround yourself with, and how they make you feel. To determine if someone is creating a positive effect on my life and in my personal growth, I try to ask myself the following questions: Do I feel inspired when I work with this person? Do I feel good about myself when I have conversations with this person? Does this person talk about ideas and change? Although I can promise I don't run through this checklist every time I meet someone new (that would be weird), these questions have been surprisingly accurate in helping me determine which individuals help me grow as a person. In a similar manner to Stephanie, the people I have chosen to associate with have been ones who have supported me, collaborated with me, and served as strong confidants.

Stephanie is changing the face of health care and serves as a true inspiration for female entrepreneurs. She is a perfect example of someone who has acknowledged a disparity in the world, and is now using her background and experience to combat it.

KEY TAKEAWAYS:
- You have the ability to make a change in flawed systems within society. Take note of your surroundings, and use your observations as an impetus for change.
- Critical, honest feedback from mentors is crucial for individual growth. Reach out to your mentors who support your mission and share your goals for success so they can help you grow.

- The people you surround yourself with can make a huge impact in your journey. Make sure the people you collaborate with are positive individuals who support your mission.

CHAPTER 15

THE ERA OF SUSTAINABLE FASHION

———

Is the fashion industry dominated by men or women?

If someone told me last year I could win one million dollars if I answered this question correctly, I would play "A Thousand Miles" by Vanessa Carlton and start making a list of every single Gucci bag I wanted. Men are omnipresent in STEM, finance, journalism, manufacturing, politics, media, and literally every other industry. Fashion is where we women have the power, right?

Lol. Wrong.

In the overarching world of fashion, from an outsider's perspective, it appears women have a huge voice. Designers target women for new trends, styles, and products. When you go to the mall, you're surrounded by women. At runway shows, designers hope young female celebrities are seen sporting their attire. Furthermore, while buying clothes and jewelry, most of the people who help you pick out outfits are women.

Although women make up about 80 percent of fashion-related purchasing decisions, according to FashionUnited.com, only 12.5 percent of apparel companies on the *Fortune* 1000 list are actually led by women.[247] In an industry that revolves around the opinions and trends of women, men make the final decisions and steer the direction of major fashion companies.

In the fashion start-up space, female founders also face tremendous obstacles. While fundraising, female fashion founders typically have to pitch their ideas to a group of investors who are almost always predominately male.

In a Glossy.com article entitled "When female fashion founders meet mansplaining VCs," Susan Naci, a partner at venture capital firm 32 Laight Street Partners, states, "You have to work a little bit harder, typically, as a woman with a fashion startup because there is some bias that still exists."[248] Susan has direct experience in the venture capital world, and as a female partner in a male-dominated field, she has firsthand insight toward the way her male colleagues think.

The *Glossy* article also dives into how the retail industry is risky for venture capital firms, "as it's a category dominated by long-established players and dependent on the retail

---

247 Marjorie van Elven, "Why is it so hard for women to become CEOs in fashion companies?" *Fashion United*, May 8, 2019.

248 Hilary Milnes, "When female fashion founders meet mansplaining VCs," *Glossy*, September 29, 2016.

climate, unlike categories like health care and software."[249] Even though females comprise the majority of retail consumers, it is still extremely difficult to convince panels of male investors that retail, beauty, or fashion products are worth their time and money.

On top of the obstacles female entrepreneurs already face in the start-up process, they must work twice as hard to nail their pitch, attract investors, and prove their concept is worth pursuing. To highlight the entirety of the start-up process for young, female entrepreneurs, I will dive into the story of Caroline Danehy, the entrepreneur who turned plastic bottles into sustainable swimwear.

SAVING THE OCEAN THROUGH SWIMWEAR—THE STORY OF CAROLINE DANEHY:

I had the chance to speak with Caroline Danehy, a savvy entrepreneur who is establishing a new world of sustainable swimwear at only twenty-two years old. Caroline is the current chief creative officer and co-founder of Fair Harbor, a swimwear company selling swimsuits made from plastic bottle waste.

Growing up, Caroline recognized the amount of plastic waste surrounding her childhood home in Fair Harbor, New York was continuously increasing. In the close-knit environment near to Fire Island, residents were seen biking, surfing, and enjoying long walks on the beach, but the increase of waste from plastic bottles was very noticeable and disappointing.

---

249 Ibid.

"When my family and I would walk down the beach that is basically a 'glorified sand bar,' waste continued to accumulate on the shore. We saw a lot of plastic bottles washed up, disturbing the natural beauty of our childhood home," says Caroline.

As Caroline continued to observe the waste levels surrounding her home increasing, her passion for helping the environment reached new heights. Soon enough, Caroline and her older brother Jake tried to figure out how they could directly solve this problem. When Caroline was only a senior in high school and Jake was a student at Colgate University, the idea behind Fair Harbor was born.

After collaborating with her brother about the different ways to mitigate the waste surrounding their beloved childhood home, Caroline and Jake discovered plastic bottles could be recycled into a certain type of polyester, and this polyester could then be transformed into apparel.

With Caroline's background in fashion and geography, and her brother's background studying the chemical aspect of the polymer, they held the individual tools to come together and launch initial prototypes. A swimwear line using polymer from plastic bottles was something that had never been done before, and they had the skills to design their own unique patterns for the suits.

After pitching their unique idea at an entrepreneurship competition to a panel of renowned creators including Jessica Alba, MC Hammer, Neil Blumenthal, and Jennifer Hyman, the powerful sibling duo received the funding they needed to take their platform to the next level.[250]

Soon after the competition, Caroline began her studies at Colgate, where she balanced the start of Fair Harbor with all of her school work as a geography major.

"When I started studying at Colgate University, I became a geography major so I could further explore how we are continuously engaging in a globalized world," says Caroline.

Adapting this mentality, Caroline continued to work as both a start-up founder and full-time college student, going from important business meetings to sorority formals.

After many different iterations of the swimwear products, the launch of three seasonal stores, and continuous pitching of the company mission to people across the United States, Fair Harbor has become rapidly successful.[251] What began as two teenagers recognizing an issue in their environment evolved into a powerful brand that large corporations should take the lead from in understanding sustainable development.

THE BENEFITS AND CHALLENGES YOUNG, FEMALE ENTREPRENEURS EXPERIENCE:
We live in a world where many college students believe entrepreneurs are born after years of experience, whether that

---

250 "Fair Harbor," *Forbes*, accessed July 16, 2020.
251 "About Us," Fair Harbor, accessed July 15, 2020.

means spending time in a corporate role at an established company, or in a period of self-discovery.

According to Robert Phillips, senior lecturer at the University of Manchester, 4.7 percent of recent UK college graduates are self-employed, and only 0.6 percent of college graduates have already started their own businesses.[252]

Caroline falls into a very small category of college students who have gone through the immense effort of building a business plan, finding investors, reiterating the product, and then launching it, all while balancing a full course load.

Although universities all around the world have launched entrepreneurship initiatives, start-up incubators, entrepreneurial mentorship programs, and different types of workshops, the number of students who actually pursue entrepreneurship straight out of college remains very low. Some of the reasons behind this include young people like the job security a corporate role can grant them, while entrepreneurship can be an emotionally and physically taxing journey, and funding is always a concern.

In a society where only 0.6 percent of recent college graduates are launching their own ventures, what is going through the minds of the 0.6 percent?[253] I asked Caroline to provide insight toward her own entrepreneurial process to see if I could get an answer to this question.

---

252 Robert Phillips, "Why do so few university graduates start their own businesses?" *The Guardian*, December 14, 2018.
253 Ibid.

"When Jake and I decided to launch Fair Harbor, it was really just a leap of faith we both decided to take. I had never made a resume or been in the corporate setting when deciding to launch Fair Harbor, and when we started working on it, it all came pretty naturally," says Caroline.

The "leap of faith" Caroline refers to took place while she was still a senior in high school. Because she started her entrepreneurial career so early, she had the opportunity to see the benefits of entrepreneurship while still being a full-time college student.

"At Fair Harbor so far, I have had immense opportunity to see how a business operates. I have honestly learned much more than I ever would have in a corporate role," says Caroline.

In an interview with *Thrive Global*, Caroline spoke about the bootstrapping process behind her company. When Fair Harbor initially launched, the sibling duo would go to small beach towns, pitching their product to anyone who would listen to their story.[254] The duo had to build a reputation to find manufacturers, continue improving their product, and establish a consumer base.[255]

Last year, Fair Harbor had two million dollars in revenue, and the company has recycled over three million water bottles to date. This is incredibly important to Caroline, as she began her mission with the goal of eliminating as much waste

254 Yitzi Weiner, "'Know the Importance of Bootstrapping' 5 Startup Strategies with Caroline Danehy, Co-Founder of Fair Harbor Clothing," *Thrive Global*, February 26, 2018.

255 Ibid.

as she could from places like her childhood home. As Fair Harbor continues to grow, Caroline continues to promote sustainable development and the preservation of natural beauty.

CAROLINE'S ADVICE FOR YOUNG, FEMALE ENTREPRENEURS:

While speaking with Caroline, she offered valuable insight for young, female entrepreneurs, and women in the workplace.

"If you walk into a meeting and you do not know something, don't be afraid to raise your hand and ask questions. When I had questions about how plastic bottles could be transformed into polymer, I would always ask the manufacturers questions," says Caroline.

Caroline explained that in her personal experience, a major component of building her confidence was actually attributed to what she didn't know. In situations when she stood up for herself and asked questions, she grew more knowledgeable and confident about her abilities to talk about the company. Caroline emphasized sometimes it is better to walk into a situation without knowing a lot. This enables you to constantly learn new things.

As a college student, I have also learned how important it is to ask questions about what you don't understand, and to constantly seek out new knowledge. Throughout my education, I have always been the student who raises my hand multiple times in lectures, or attends office hours each week. This has led to me being called a try-hard, or an overachiever, in more instances than I can count. Initially, being called these names led me to avoid asking too many questions, fearing that other students would think negatively of me. Although it took me a few years to change this mindset, I ultimately discovered why this takes place. When people call others "try-hard" or "overachiever," it typically stems from their own insecurity. Additionally, if no one is trying hard, or "overachieving," this means the society we live in remains average.

I have learned that the greatest thinkers, innovators, and game-changers in society are ones who ask questions, go above and beyond, and unapologetically pursue their missions. Without people like Caroline who work extremely hard, and constantly seek out new knowledge, the world remains stagnant.

Caroline's emphasis on finding mentors and asking plenty of questions falls in direct correlation with an issue many women in the workplace face: not wanting to ask for help.

Unlike Allegra, "the Soloist," Caroline views asking questions as a means to push herself forward, rather than hold herself back.[256] She does not think asking for help makes her look less intelligent or competent. If Caroline had not asked questions in meetings, she would not have been able to speak as confidently as she can now about the manufacturing side of Fair Harbor.

---

256 Valerie Young, *The Secret Thoughts of Successful Women: Why Capable People Suffer from the Impostor Syndrome and How to Thrive in Spite of It*, (New York: Crown Business, 2011).

Additionally, Caroline emphasized that her personal entrepreneurial journey was a continual self-discovery process.

"We are humans, so it is so important to ask questions, be curious, and embrace the process," says Caroline. Rather than chasing after perfection, Caroline has embraced every step of the process in founding Fair Harbor, and this has driven her success.

Through maintaining authenticity, asking questions, building connections, and embracing the entrepreneurial journey, Caroline has established herself as a trailblazer for young women interested in launching their own start-ups in college.

As far as the next steps go, Caroline is continuing to build Fair Harbors' unique platform and growth model. Her pathway truly highlights resilience and self-discovery, and she is shaping the world of entrepreneurship as we know it.

KEY TAKEAWAYS:
- Use what you don't know to your advantage. When you enter uncertain situations, raise your hand, ask for help, and build connections. Open yourself up to new insight that can transform your mindset.
- You are never too young to launch a unique brand, idea, or concept into the world.
- Sometimes, acknowledging things you want to change in your own backyard can inspire brands, ideas, and products. Listen to your intuition, and learn from the world around you.

CHAPTER 16

BUILDING BRANDS AND BECOMING BOSSES

—

If you have ever turned on your TV on a Saturday night, you have probably seen the iconic "Jake from State Farm" commercial. A middle-aged man is on the phone with someone late at night and says, "Yeah, I'm married. Does it matter?" All of the sudden, his wife comes downstairs and asks who he is speaking to. He says, "It's Jake from State Farm." When the wife takes the phone, she asks what Jake is wearing. The State Farm employee on the line hesitantly says "Uhm…khakis."[257]

This commercial strategically uses comedy to make the world of insurance a bit more interesting. This has promoted State Farm's "Like a Good Neighbor" campaign tremendously, and it has built the company's brand even further.[258]

---

257 State Farm Insurance, "Back in the Office | State Farm," February 2, 2020, YouTube video.

258 Ibid.

In 2010, Snickers came out with their iconic series of "You're not you when you're hungry" commercials.[259] In the original "You're not you when you're hungry" commercial, they featured a thirty-year-old man transforming into Betty White when his appetite took over in the middle of a football game.[260] Snickers has used this campaign for over ten years now, and it continues to build its customer base.[261]

Wendy's social media marketing team has turned its image from a wholesome, family-friendly brand represented by a young girl with pigtails to a completely savage and hilarious brand via Twitter. In January 2017, when a Twitter follower asked how much a Big Mac costs, Wendy's reply was, "Your dignity."[262] In the same month, a follower tagged Wendy's account saying "BK for the win," referencing Wendy's competitor, Burger King.[263] Immediately, Wendy's account shot back saying, "What'd they win? A participation trophy."[264] Fast forward a few years to when Popeyes came out with a new chicken sandwich in 2019. When this happened, Wendy's did not miss the chance to roast the brand's attempt at creating an iconic new menu item.[265]

---

259 Yannick Bikker, "You're Not You When You're Hungry: The Best Ad Campaign Ever?" *Medium*, March 21, 2020.

260 Ibid.

261 Ibid.

262 LMA, "Wendy's Is Roasting People on Twitter, and It's Just Too Funny," *Bored Panda.*

263 Ibid.

264 Ibid.

265 Kate Taylor, "Wendy's jumps into the chicken-sandwich Twitter feud between Popeyes and Chick-fil-A," *Business Insider*, August 20, 2019.

After seeing the commotion over a chicken sandwich on Twitter, I have to admit I waited in the hour-long line in the ninety-degree heat just to see if the sandwich lived up to its hype. (Spoiler alert: it did not. Chick-fil-A is still superior.) But the point is—the marketing tactics used by fast-food media accounts drew me in and led me to take an hour out of my day to try a new product. I did not take the time out of my day to try the chicken sandwich because I thought it was going to be the best chicken sandwich of my life. I wanted to try it because so many people were talking about it, and this piqued my curiosity.

Marketing and advertising are major facets of all companies, and they can steer a company's branding, image, overall message, and customer base in endless directions. Marketing can make consumers laugh, cry, feel empowered, feel angry, or all of the above. The individuals sitting in marketing seats have the ability to set the company's tone, and to establish the company's image that will be broadcasted to the public.

I had the unique opportunity to interview two different women who have truly dominated the field of marketing and were both named on the *Forbes* 30 Under 30 list in marketing and advertising. These women truly embody excellence and provide valuable lessons about achieving your goals. I will first dive into the story behind Arielle Gross Samuels, the head of global business strategy and engagement at Facebook. Then, I will highlight the story of Thea Neal, the former lead social media strategist for Hallmark Gold Crown stores and current talent marketing manager for Royal Caribbean Group.

FEMALE CMOS ARE KILLING THE GAME:

Before discussing the stories of Arielle and Thea, it is important to take a step back and to look at female representation in the marketing industry as a whole. In the marketing industry, the voices of women with power are shining. In 2019, *Forbes* released a report entitled this year's "World's Most Influential CMOs."[266] This list was used "to assess the extent to which CMOs are using their voices, visibility, stature, and decisions for change in three areas: inside their companies, in the broader advertising and marketing industry, and in society and culture, at a time when corporations are now regarded by many as the most powerful social forces."[267] On the list of "The World's Most Influential CMOs," thirty-one out of the top fifty CMOs featured are women, and nineteen are men.[268]

Despite the lack of female representation at many top firms and companies, in the marketing world, women are rising to the top and doing really well at it.

In the *Forbes* article titled "The World's Most Influential CMOs 2019," Kristin Lemkau is praised for her work promoting the #ThisMama campaign as CMO of JPMorgan Chase.[269] The #ThisMama campaign stars Serena Williams, an international icon known for her success in the tennis world.[270] This campaign champions females who balance

---

266 Jenny Rooney, "The World's Most Influential CMOs 2019," *Forbes*, June 20, 2019.
267 Ibid.
268 Ibid.
269 Ibid.
270 Ibid.

motherhood and career success, and brings many important topics about females in the workplace to light.[271]

The mid-career gap between males and females is oftentimes attributed to women leaving their roles for maternity leave and not returning. Through campaigns like #ThisMama, a greater sense of community is established amongst women who are working that have children, or women who are on leave and want to re-enter the workforce.[272]

Although Arielle and Thea work in marketing for completely different companies (Royal Caribbean could not be more different than Facebook), their approaches to success share many similarities.

ARIELLE GROSS SAMUELS—CHANGING THE GAME FOR MARKETING WHIZZES ACROSS THE GLOBE:
"If not now, when? If not me, who?"

When I asked what has helped Arielle become such a successful leader at Facebook, she used this quote her mother constantly told her growing up. This quote emphasizes you should continue to try and reach your goals as you see new opportunities for yourself. Now is the time. You must have faith in yourself and your abilities.

Although Arielle is now a marketing queen at Facebook, she has developed her career through having exposure to many

---

271 Ibid.
272 Ibid.

different industries. While Arielle was at University of Illinois at Urbana-Champaign, she studied materials science and engineering. During her college years, she held internships at Procter & Gamble in R&D, and in technical prototyping. Upon graduation, Arielle pursued engineering and construction consulting at Deloitte for a brief period. From 2013 forward, she has worked at Facebook, and now serves as the head of global business strategy and engagement.

"I've found it really rewarding to try on different hats and solve a breadth of problems—from product operations to global creative programs to business marketing partnerships. It helps me connect dots faster when I'm exposed to more challenges and opportunities," says Arielle.

As head of global business strategy and engagement, Arielle leads strategy, business, communication, and management initiatives for Facebook's global business marketing and creative shop organizations.[273] In this role, she leads a marketing team focused on social impact, trust, advocacy, and diversity for over one hundred eighty million businesses around the world.[274] She is currently leading Facebook's initiative to support Black-owned businesses impacted by COVID-19 by providing over forty million dollars in grants to over ten thousand Black-owned businesses in the US. In addition to her role at Facebook, Arielle recently joined the board of the Geena Davis Institute of Gender in Media, focusing on the elimination of harmful bias in the media we consume.

---

273 "Arielle Gross Samuels," LinkedIn, accessed September 15, 2020.
274 Ibid.

Arielle champions diversity, female empowerment, and social change, and she uses her platform to promote these causes. Arielle is particularly known for founding the Connected events series and helping launch the #MoreLikeMe initiative in partnership with HP Inc., two platforms promoting diversity and inclusivity in the workplace.[275]

The Connected events series was inspired by the Cannes Lions International Festival of Creativity, one of the biggest marketing conferences in the world.[276] It is located in Cannes, France amongst dreamy beaches, exclusive parties, and the most exquisite French food you could ever think of.[277] As you can probably guess, getting to Cannes is not easy. You have to book tickets, book a hotel, shop for outfits, and clear your entire work schedule those days.

Understanding that this platform inevitably excludes bright people in the marketing and advertising industry who cannot afford or make it to the festival, Arielle took it upon herself to make this event more inclusive. Arielle decided to launch the Connected event series in New York, London, São Paulo, Sydney, and Johannesburg, cities with a high population of marketing agencies.[278] At these locations, Arielle planned fireside chats with innovative leaders like Bobbi Brown, fun parties with DJs, networking events, and even creative

275 Ilyse Liffreing, "Facebook is hosting 'Connected' events around the world for creatives who can't make it to Cannes Lions," *Campaign Live*, June 14, 2017.

276 Ibid.

277 Ibid.

278 Ibid.

platforms for exercise.[279] She helped deliver these events so that they were just like the festival in Cannes, only free and more accessible.

In addition to her role in jumpstarting the Cannected event series, Arielle is well-known for helping launch Facebook's #MoreLikeMe initiative in partnership with HP Inc.[280] The #MoreLikeMe initiative is a mentoring program dedicated to strengthening diverse talent.[281] The leaders of this initiative selected a handful of racially and ethnically diverse stars from lead agency partners across the UK, US, and Mexico to attend the 2018 Cannes Lions International Festival of Creativity.[282] Following this festival, #MoreLikeMe provided the participants with long-term mentors and leadership opportunities.[283]

Rather than just talking about why diversity and inclusivity is important in the workplace, Arielle is tackling this issue headfirst. She has found ways to provide creative people in the marketing industry a voice, and she has found ways to train and develop talent, so that the marketing pipeline becomes more diverse over time.

WHY ARIELLE'S PATH IS SO IMPORTANT:
As Arielle continues to build her platform at Facebook, she continues to empower females, ethnic minorities, under-

---

279 Ibid.
280 "HP #MoreLikeMe," Edelman, accessed September 25, 2020.
281 Ibid.
282 Ibid.
283 Ibid.

represented communities, and young people entering the marketing world. But she has inevitably faced challenges along the way.

When I asked Arielle about the greatest challenge she has faced in her career so far, she said it was tied to "not having a playbook."

"A lot of the work I do, and that the company generally does, is unprecedented. Without a guide or set of pre-existing tutorials, the work can sometimes be intimidating, but I've found I can also do some of my best work through building proposals, trying different solutions, iterating and learning," says Arielle.

Arielle stresses the power of unconventionality. She emphasizes having a set pathway and knowing exactly what you're doing isn't always the most important priority. According to Jeffrey Baumgartner, the author of *The Way of the Innovation Master*, "your goal is not to generate as many ideas as possible in hopes a few will be good ideas. Your goal is to generate a few unconventional ideas which could make a big difference."[284] Arielle emphasizes if you are not unconventional in your pursuits, you are not maximizing your creative and innovative potential.

Arielle also emphasizes the importance of mastering the interview. Because Arielle has worked in many different industries and held many different roles, she has had to go

---

284 Jeffrey Baumgartner, "When you Need Breakthrough Ideas, Consider Anti-conventional Thinking," *Innovation Management*.

through many different interviews. Each time, she has had to showcase her talents and win over new people. She highlights that communication and confidence can be equally, if not more important than checking off boxes in a job description or having certain technical skills on a resume.

"For my different career shifts I've interviewed each time—selling people on my skills and vision, articulating the value I would bring to their team and problem space, and manifesting curiosity in studying up on their work, and asking informed questions," says Arielle.

Arielle explains how interviewing is a unique opportunity to practice talking about your skills to shine, and she encourages all young people to work on their interview skills.

Without even realizing it at first, everything Arielle spoke about was completely applicable to my life as well. In my job search process, the most amazing opportunities have resulted from networking and building connections with people in industry. When it was time for interviews, I viewed them as unique opportunities to reflect on everything I've accomplished. In the past, I worried about coming across as too braggy or cocky if I talked about all of my achievements. Many of my peers in college have expressed these same concerns as well. It is often hard to determine the extent to which talking about our accomplishments goes from normal and confident, to cocky and annoying.

Arielle has helped me realize that showcasing your accomplishments does not make you cocky; it makes you confident, and empowered. Arielle preaches that all young people are capable and competent, and interviews are times for you to reflect what you've done, reflect why you want to work at the company, and to express that you want to continue to grow.

Rather than saying, "Yes, I won this award, but it wasn't a huge deal," you should say, "I won this award because of my hard work and passion for (insert field)."

Arielle continues to shape the face of the marketing industry, bringing in new talent, creating opportunities for more diversity, while also building her career and her voice. She is a powerful mentor, role model, and businesswoman, and her pathway highlights why you should never shy away from arenas where you can embrace your creativity and voice.

THEA NEAL—THE STORY BEHIND THE SELF-PROCLAIMED LOVECHILD OF SHERYL SANDBERG AND RIHANNA:

Under the same overarching umbrella of marketing, Thea Neal, the former lead social media strategist for Hallmark Gold Crown stores and current talent marketing manager for all of Royal Caribbean Group, has used her voice to make an impact upon and transform the marketing world.

Thea Neal's passionate attitude, zest for life, and strong positivity are vastly evident in her demeanor.

"Eat dessert. I've never eaten a dessert I've regretted," she says in an interview with *The Kansas City Star*.[285]

---

285 Jared Bajkowski, "Meet the Hallmark social media pro who just made Forbes' 30 Under 30 list," *The Kansas City Star*, November 30, 2017.

Even in her LinkedIn bio, Thea says she is "the ultimate result if Rihanna and Sheryl Sandberg met at a social media conference and had a love child with a penchant for bold accessories and driving ROI."[286]

Thea was named on the *Forbes* 30 Under 30 list after revolutionizing the world of marketing for Hallmark stores all over the world. In her first year at Hallmark, she initiated partnerships with new, innovative influencers, becoming an instrumental force behind Hallmark's appeal to a young, new sensational audience. According to Thea's feature on *Forbes*, her work with influencers generated three million user engagements and over fifty million impressions in the very first year she started working.[287] In the marketing world, this is absolutely phenomenal. When someone from a brand's target audience sees an advertisement, this signifies an impression in marketing.[288] Impressions are vastly used across companies to build brand awareness and establish a larger customer base, particularly in digital marketing.[289]

In addition to Thea's tremendous work in collaborating with new minds to promote Hallmark's mission, she served as the sensational host of "Party 101." "Party 101" is just as exciting as it sounds. From making rainbow cupcake inspirations to Halloween cocktails, "Party 101's" bright, creative, outlook is widely representative of Thea's impact on Hallmark. Whether you were trying to come up with last minute activities for

---

286 "Thea Neal," LinkedIn, accessed September 15, 2020.
287 "Thea Neal," *Forbes*, accessed September 15, 2020.
288 "Understanding Impressions in digital marketing," Big Commerce, accessed September 16, 2020.
289 Ibid.

your child's tenth birthday party, or add a spunky, waterless terrarium to your college dorm room, "Party 101" was there to help. This platform generated a huge Hallmark community built on the premise of collaboration and creativity. Thea's unique videos drew in over two hundred thousand views, and over $25,000 in sales at Hallmark stores across the United States.[290]

After leaving a lasting impact on Hallmark, Thea accepted a role at Royal Caribbean, where she currently manages the global marketing operations for talent attraction across Royal Caribbean International, Celebrity Cruises, Azamara, and Silversea Cruises.

CHALLENGING AND OVERCOMING THE IMPOSTOR:
As soon as Thea entered the marketing world, she tackled the industry head-on. After being recruited at Hallmark, she used innovative branding tools to make a lasting impact upon the company.

"When I entered Hallmark, Instagram wasn't huge, and a lot of people had the impression Hallmark's target audience was older people. Seeing there was a whole audience of 'mom-lle-neals' I could appeal to, I knew this could be a phenomenal opportunity for me to build Hallmark's social media platform," says Thea.

But, the part about Thea's story that stood out to me the most was not tied to the number of hits her advertising tactics

---

290 "Thea Neal," *Forbes*, accessed September 15, 2020.

received, or how she led Hallmark to success. The most meaningful part of her story was how she broke free from Impostor Syndrome.

Thea Neal experienced Impostor Syndrome when she was initially named onto the *Forbes* 30 Under 30 list. In a LinkedIn post, she opened up about her internal obstacles after being named on the iconic list, and how she overcame them.[291]

Thea initially experienced an overwhelming sense of joy after accomplishing one of her greatest dreams: making it onto the *Forbes* 30 Under 30 list. But, then, the doubt sunk in.

"I was worried that they had made a mistake (despite the published story, emails and countless congratulations from *Forbes*)," says Thea.[292]

Thea felt like a fraud, and didn't think she deserved the award. She knew she had worked incredibly hard, but she did not think her hard work was worthy of the prominent 30 Under 30 title.

"I felt like I had magically tricked this infamous magazine into awarding me with a prestigious award that would follow me my whole life, and suddenly every ounce of confidence I had that got me to this position was totally gone," says Thea.[293]

---

291 Thea Neal, "Imposter Syndrome, or what I faced after being named to Forbes 30 Under 30," *LinkedIn*, November 27, 2017.

292 Ibid.

293 Ibid.

Once the congratulations from her friends, family, and colleagues came in, Thea's Impostor Syndrome manifested even further. According to Thea, she was inevitably concerned with appearing "too braggy," even though she had worked hard and had rightfully earned her spot onto the list.[294] When people congratulated her, she responded with the same response, "Thank you so much; yeah, it's so weird!"[295]

It ultimately took a meeting with a high school friend for Thea to realize she earned her spot onto the list, she was confident in herself, and it *was* a big deal.[296] She didn't need to follow up her thank you's with "it's so weird," because it wasn't weird.[297] She had worked extremely hard, and she deserved it. After further discussing this topic with her boss, she realized she had just fallen victim to Impostor Syndrome.

Thea realized despite her accomplishments, hard work, and the extensive mentorship she received from inspirational females, she still faced the internalized lack of confidence many females in the workplace experience.

When I asked her how she decided to combat these sensations, she offered meaningful advice.

"If you hold yourself back, no one will advocate for you. Impostor Syndrome is 100 percent self-imposed. Usually, the biggest person holding you back is yourself. Rather than letting this happen, remind yourself of all of your

---

294 Ibid.
295 Ibid.
296 Ibid.
297 Ibid.

accomplishments, and remind yourself you worked hard, and you deserve everything that comes to you. It is totally okay to be proud of your accomplishments and own your talents—this doesn't make you braggy," says Thea.

Thea's story directly connects to Rachel, "The Superwoman."[298] Rachel works part-time at an investment bank, she is a full-time student, and she maintains an extensive list of extracurricular activities. Although she is able to balance so many impressive activities, she still does not feel competent.

In response to the circumstances experienced as part of "The Superwoman" archetype, Thea challenged herself to tackle her internal lack of confidence. Even though this took a sit-down lunch with her boss and high school friend to acknowledge why she was feeling down, she ultimately used her realization as a platform to grow stronger. Sometimes, to overcome internal obstacles, sitting down with mentors and confidants who believe in you is what it takes to bring your confidence and strength back.

Thea also emphasizes how overcoming Impostor Syndrome can be done in many different ways in the workforce while seeking higher pay and promotions.

"As women, when we have to ask for raises, it's scary. But, it is so important we acknowledge our worth and go for it. If we don't speak up for ourselves, who will?" says Thea.

---

298 Valerie Young, *The Secret Thoughts of Successful Women: Why Capable People Suffer from the Impostor Syndrome and How to Thrive in Spite of It*, (New York: Crown Business, 2011).

Thea is absolutely right. In the workforce, mentors and sponsors are extremely important, but it is ultimately up to you to advocate for yourself. You must be your biggest cheerleader and supporter and acknowledge you can do great things.

Both Thea and Arielle demonstrate that we must stand up for ourselves to reach success, even if it falls outside of our comfort zones.

Thea and Arielle's positive attitudes and leadership skills have continued to help them succeed. Through encouraging the next generation of millennial women to be authentic, innovative, and unique, they are continuing to use their platforms to build confidence and leadership skills amongst young women all across the world.

KEY TAKEAWAYS:
- Master the art of the interview. Sell people on your skills and vision, and articulate the value you would bring to their team or problem space. It doesn't matter if you don't meet all of the "minimum requirements" of the job. You got this.
- If you're hard working and good things happen to you, it didn't happen because of luck. NEVER think it happened because of luck.
- Trial and error is a key element of success. You're not going to come up with an award-winning solution unless you try many different processes and iterate.

PART THREE

THE GRAND FINALE

CHAPTER 17

OWNING THE IMPOSTOR

———

Last night before going to bed, I thought long and hard about how I would conclude this book. After brushing my teeth, doing my nightly skincare routine, and hopping into bed, I recounted all of the stories I have heard, all of the people I have met, and the most impactful events I have experienced in life.

Ironically enough, one of the most transformative accounts that has shaped my mindset is the story of how my cousin Niko from Greece accidentally made it onto his high school soccer team.

When my cousin Niko was a freshman in high school, he was shorter than the rest of his peers, slightly clumsy, and ate three doughnuts a day after school (I don't blame him—his dad runs a restaurant and always had leftovers). Although my cousin was not the most athletic nor the most agile in his abilities, he tried out for the soccer team with the rest of his friends.

On the last day of tryouts, they posted the final roster on the board with everyone who made the team listed in red. Seeing the name "Niko" in bold letters, my cousin was ecstatic. To his complete shock, he made it onto the team.

Soon enough, Niko had greater faith in himself and in his abilities. He stayed after practice each day for forty-five minutes to repeat drills and woke up at five o'clock each morning to go through sprint routines. He became a powerhouse for the team, and slowly became known as their "secret weapon."

At the end of his senior year, he was recognized as one of the most influential members the team ever had.

During the senior banquet, his coach pulled him to the side and revealed shocking news.

"You know Niko…I created the roster for the team, and when I wrote Niko, I wasn't talking about you. I was talking about Niko Pappas. The next morning when I saw you at practice an hour before everyone else, I decided to give you another shot. I'm so happy I did."

In this moment, my cousin realized his ability to succeed was something he was capable of the entire time; he just had to believe in himself. He realized anyone is capable of reaching their full potential, they have to have faith in their abilities and prove to themselves they can achieve greatness.

I am not including this story to encourage you to try and forge a spot onto a sports team or to imply that it is easy to change your entire mindset in life when one thing goes your way. But I do want this story to highlight how your internal perception of yourself influences your ability to achieve your goals.

Growing up, I was not always the most confident student. I distinctly remember one day in sixth grade social studies where we had to write letters to the president. Before sending these letters out, we had to peer edit other students' letters for feedback on grammar and structure. I remember not wanting to let any other students read my letter, fearing I would be "exposed" as a terrible writer.

As time went on, I continued to worry and worry about my writing abilities until the end of high school. At the end of high school, I was named valedictorian of my class. Despite having worked extremely hard for four years to accomplish this, I did not want to give the speech. I did not think I could appeal to the entire audience, and quite honestly, I thought I would pass out on stage in front of everyone.

On the morning of June 17, 2017, I stood proudly in front of hundreds of people at the Time Warner Cable Arena. While relaying the accomplishments of my grade and how hard we had worked, I used my voice to connect with each and every person in the audience. I ended the speech with a quote from my all-time favorite movie, *Legally Blonde.*

"It is with passion, courage of conviction, and strong sense of self that we take our next steps into the world, remembering that first impressions are not always correct. You must always have faith in people, and most importantly, you must always have faith in yourself."[299]

After ending the speech with this quote, the crowd erupted with applause. In this moment, I realized the stigma I held toward public speaking, and sharing my writing was entirely an internal battle.

After realizing this, I decided to brand myself in the most authentic version possible, using three words as my personal weapons:

Brains: you are intelligent and capable of creating ideas, and inspiring others.

Beauty: you are internally and externally beautiful. You bring radiance and charisma to each and every situation.

Boss: when you walk into a room, you run the show. You can and will accomplish your goals.

I am now a published author and speaker, and I am incredibly proud of what I have accomplished.

---

299 "Legally Blonde," directed by Robert Luketic (2001; Beverly Hills: Metro-Goldwyn-Mayer), DVD.

THE BRAINS, BEAUTY, AND BOSS WOMEN OF THE FORBES 30 UNDER 30 LIST:

Throughout this entire book, I have described the stories of some of the most powerful women in the world. The women I had the chance to interview are transforming industries, building their names, and rising to the top. But if you haven't noticed, most of these women had to overcome internal obstacles, and "own the Impostor" within them.

At the start of this book, you were all introduced to the imaginary characters: Sarah the Perfectionist, Blair the Natural Genius, Rachel the Superwoman, Allegra the Soloist, and Hanna the Expert.[300] Although many of these characters were dramatized to fit the mold of twenty-first century millennial women, they were uniquely crafted to highlight how Impostor Syndrome has become so normalized within society.

Dr. Valerie Young introduced the competence types of the Perfectionist, the Natural Genius, the Superwoman, the Soloist, and the Expert to show the world that some of the most accomplished women still struggle with finding their strengths, and acknowledging that their achievements are worthy of being shared.[301]

According to Dr. Young, "You can have all the confidence in the world and still be reluctant to self-promote out of a

---

300 Valerie Young, *The Secret Thoughts of Successful Women: Why Capable People Suffer from the Impostor Syndrome and How to Thrive in Spite of It*, (New York: Crown Business, 2011).

301 Melody Wilding, "5 Different Types of Imposter Syndrome (and 5 Ways to Battle Each One," *The Muse*.

steadfast belief that a person's work should speak for itself. It doesn't."[302]

Dr. Young makes a point that has helped me, and can help every young woman in their career path: you are your most important advocate. You are capable of sharing your story with the world, but you are also capable of holding it back. If you are struggling with Impostor Syndrome, you have the ability to overcome it, and to own up to your abilities. When all individuals learn how to "own their Impostors," society will transform into a more innovative, inclusive, and inspiring place.

HOW SARAH, BLAIR, RACHEL, ALLEGRA, AND HANNA CONNECT TO FORBES 30 UNDER 30 WOMEN:

You may be wondering why I created the imaginary characters of Sarah, Blair, Rachel, Allegra, and Hanna in the first place, and why I tried to tie them into interviews with women on the *Forbes* 30 Under 30 list.

After interviewing many different women on the *Forbes* 30 Under 30 list, I had exposure to unique pathways to success, and clear takeaways each woman could offer other young women entering the business world.

Soon enough, I found pieces of advice from certain interviews that could directly help women like Sarah, the

---

302 "The Secret Thoughts of Successful Women," Goodreads.com, accessed October 11, 2020.

Perfectionist.[303] I realized each woman I interviewed had very useful information that could bring Sarah, Blair, Rachel, Allegra, and Hanna closer to owning their Impostors. Obviously, I had to share this information with the world.

SARAH, THE PERFECTIONIST:[304]

Sarah, the Perfectionist, represents the woman who wants everything to fall perfectly into place. She sets extremely high expectations for herself, and she believes that what she accomplishes is never enough. To break free from this cycle, here is what she can do:

1. **Embrace the power of unconventionality:** When Lizz Warner started her job at BuzzFeed, she had no idea what to expect. When she realized there was an opportunity for her to tap into the market of online travel platforms, she began BringMe! Instead of holding herself to unrealistic expectations tied to content views and shares, she took it each day at a time, championing the "small wins." This ultimately led to BringMe! becoming rapidly successful. When you forget to praise yourself for the great things you have already accomplished, you will always chase an unrealistic idea of "perfection." You must keep in mind that imperfection and mistakes are crucial to the learning process.

2. **Allow time for self-reflection:** When Amy Odell began her career at Cosmopolitan.com, she took on the role

---

303 Valerie Young, *The Secret Thoughts of Successful Women: Why Capable People Suffer from the Impostor Syndrome and How to Thrive in Spite of It*, (New York: Crown Business, 2011).

304 Ibid.

of transforming the entire online platform of *Cosmo* to make it less about gossip and beauty standards and more about politics and female empowerment. Amy left Cosmopolitan.com because she reflected on her career there and decided that she accomplished the goal she set out to achieve. Without allowing time to reflect on everything you have done well, you will constantly think you have more to do to reach success. One way to do this is to keep positive notes for yourself. Every week, try to write down at least two amazing things you have accomplished. Whenever you are feeling uninspired, look back at these notes, and reflect on all of your wins so far.

3. **Work smarter, not harder:** When Anna Therese Day began her career as a journalist, she worked extremely hard and constantly sought out new opportunities. Anna used her work ethic to her advantage, whereas the work ethic of Perfectionists can sometimes work to their disadvantage. Anna worked hard, but she kept her end goal in mind the entire time. For example, if she wanted to document the revolution in Egypt, she connected with professors, institutions, and her personal network to make this happen. Then, she worked diligently for her stories to gain traction and appeal. Perfectionists often work longer hours and are more focused on the time they spend on their goals rather than focusing on the goals themselves. When you are working on something for a long time, always ask yourself: why am I still working on this? Am I doing anything that will improve my trajectory, or can I allocate my time to something different?

BLAIR, THE NATURAL GENIUS:[305]

Blair, the Natural Genius, represents the woman who measures competence in terms of ease and speed. She believes that if she cannot tackle a new task quickly, she is incompetent in that area. This mindset can lead to her avoiding challenges, avoiding risks, and avoiding situations where the outcome is unknown. To break free from this cycle, here is what she can do:

1. **Don't be afraid to take risks:** When Gina Kirch entered her career in the financial services industry, there had just been a major economic crisis. Finance was not the most secure industry, but she knew she had the skills and passion to succeed. After taking this initial risk, she advanced over time and became BlackRock's youngest director of all time. Gina's path highlights that if you let the fear of failure override an opportunity, you will miss your chance for something that can improve your trajectory tremendously.

2. **Remain confident in what you can and will bring to the table:** Before starting Boulder Care, Stephanie Papes had extensive exposure to the healthcare market through her previous roles, including a position at a venture capital firm that focused on healthcare companies. Stephanie acknowledged what she knew, and how she could use her knowledge to empower others. This led to her starting a company focused on making opioid care more accessible. When people who are very experienced in an area do not display confidence, this limits them from expanding their

305 Valerie Young, *The Secret Thoughts of Successful Women: Why Capable People Suffer from the Impostor Syndrome and How to Thrive in Spite of It,* (New York: Crown Business, 2011).

knowledge and expanding their abilities. If you acknowledge you are very knowledgeable in a certain area, you should remain confident in yourself, understanding you can build even more knowledge over time.

RACHEL, THE SUPERWOMAN:[306]

Rachel, the Superwoman, loads her schedule beyond its capacity. She balances many different activities, but she never truly believes that she is doing enough. Here is what she can do to break this cycle:

1. **Allow your body to reset so you can generate fresh, new ideas:** Charlie Javice is currently running an entire education technology start-up. She works long days, and constantly has new tasks on her to-do list. Instead of working nonstop, she allots one day over the weekend to herself so that she can recharge. When people do not rest, they lose focus and fall into a detrimental cycle. You should never feel bad for taking a mental health day, or for going to bed early some nights (even if you have a lot of work still to do). Maintaining a healthy work-life balance is crucial.

2. **Stay focused on what your mission is:** When I spoke with Sally Nuamah, she emphasized the importance of staying focused on your mission. When people do not stay focused on their mission, they may find themselves taking on a lot of additional work or tasks because they associate success with workload. Success is absolutely not tied to workload, and Sally made it clear that your amount or level of work means nothing in relation to

---

306 Ibid.

what your mission is. If you stay focused on your mission, you will gain confidence in the process.

3. **Have transparent conversations with your mentors:** When Thea Neal made it onto the *Forbes* 30 Under 30 list, she thought it was a huge mistake. She truly did not think she deserved this accolade, despite the fact she had accomplished great things. When Thea sat down with a mentor, she relayed her emotions to her, and her mentor helped her realize that she was experiencing Impostor Syndrome. After this conversation, Thea realized she was being way too hard on herself and she deserved her spot on the *Forbes* 30 Under 30 list. If you ever feel inadequate, it is crucial that you communicate with mentors, or people who you trust. Oftentimes, these people can shape your entire outlook, as they are not experiencing the same internal struggles you're facing.

ALLEGRA, THE SOLOIST:[307]

Allegra, the Soloist, avoids asking for help. She thinks asking for help is a sign of incompetence. She is also accustomed to being very independent, and she associates independence with success. Here is what she can do to break this mindset:

1. **You have to be honest with what you don't know:** When Megan O'Connor was starting Nth Cycle, she did not have an MBA, or any form of a business background. Instead of trying to tackle the business component of Nth Cycle all on her own, she sought out advice from people with business backgrounds. This knowledge enabled her company to have a strong business model. If you are not

---

307 Ibid.

honest with what you don't know, it will only hurt you in the long-run. Asking for help is a completely natural process, and it needs to become more normalized. Don't be afraid to slide into someone's DMs (on LinkedIn, that is), research terms you have no idea exist, or even reach out to old professors. Most people usually want to offer guidance or can connect you with others who can help you. (If not—the worst thing that happens is they say no).

2. **Use what you don't know to your advantage:** When Caroline Danehy launched Fair Harbor, she was still in high school. She had very little insight about the manufacturing process behind her swimwear products, and she constantly raised her hand in meetings with manufacturers to learn more about this. This ultimately helped her tremendously because in future business meetings and pitches, she could speak confidently about the manufacturing process with knowledge she had acquired. Raising her hand and gaining firsthand knowledge helped build Caroline's confidence as a young entrepreneur.

HANNA, THE EXPERT:[308]

Hanna, the Expert, knows a lot about a topic, but never thinks she knows enough. She feels like an Impostor when people claim she is an expert in a certain subject area. Here is what she can do to break this mindset:

1. **Raise your hand, even if you aren't sure about your answer:** When Sarah Filman began her job at Microsoft, she did not raise her hand in meetings unless she thought her answer was absolutely correct. Oftentimes, she was

---

308 Ibid.

right—her confidence was just standing in the way. If you raise your hand every single time you are asked a question you think you know the answer to, you will become more comfortable sharing your insight. Soon enough, you will have more faith in your knowledge as an "Expert" in an area.

2. **Take an idea and run with it:** When Arsheen Allam was developing the initial ideas for her start-ups, she conducted extensive research on graphene. Instead of stressing over what she did not know about graphene, she decided to move forward with her concept. Rather than fearing you are not an "Expert," you should take leaps of faith as early as you can, acknowledging what you do know. If you remain in constant fear that you don't know enough, then you will reach your goal. The best entrepreneurs do not become experts in an area before launching a concept. They learn through experience and iterating ideas over time.

OWN THE IMPOSTOR:

In the same manner I have outlined how Sarah, Blair, Rachel, Allegra, and Hanna can overcome their internal Impostors, and maximize their full potentials, I would like the same to apply to each and every person who reads this book.

As women enter the workforce, there are a multitude of forces against them that are not under their control. As I outlined in each chapter, there are many positive changes being made, but there is still a long, uphill battle ahead concerning gender equality in the workplace.

Despite these circumstances, overcoming Impostor Syndrome and overcoming internal obstacles is something that lies entirely in our hands. You have the power to create opportunities and to redefine your story. Tina Fey did it after working as a receptionist, Meryl Streep did it after being rejected time after time, and Lizzo did it after living out of her car.

You have the brains, you have the beauty, and you are a boss. Now, go after it.

CHAPTER 18

APPENDIX

CHAPTER 1

Bright Side. "15 Women Who Became Successful Later in Life and Proved It's Never Too Late." Accessed July 25, 2020. https://brightside.me/wonder-people/15-women-who-became-successful-later-in-life-and-proved-its-never-too-late-796291/.

Cosmopolitan.com. "Get That Life." Accessed July 25, 2020.

Factinate. "41 Rocking Facts About Tina Fey." Accessed July 25, 2020. https://www.factinate.com/people/41-rocking-facts-tina-fey/.

Forbes. "Meet the Top Young Entrepreneurs of the Forbes Under 30 2020 List." Accessed July 3, 2020.

Haden, Jeff. "17 Great Sheryl Sandberg Quotes on Success, Leadership, and Perseverance." Inc.com, March 30, 2018. https://www.inc.com/jeff-haden/17-great-sheryl-sandberg-quotes-on-success-leadership-perseverance.html.

Harriet, Alexander. "Meryl Streep told she was 'too ugly' to act in King Kong." *The Telegraph*, November 11, 2015. https://www. telegraph.co.uk/news/worldnews/northamerica/usa/11988870/ Meryl-Streep-told-she-was-too-ugly-to-act-in-King-Kong. html.

Mohr, Tara. "Why Women Don't Apply for Jobs Unless They're 100% Qualified." *Harvard Business Review*, August 25, 2014. https://hbr.org/2014/08/why-women-dont-apply-for-jobs-un- less-theyre-100-qualified.

Narins, Elizabeth. "Get That Life: How I Became the CEO of SoulCycle." *Cosmopolitan.com*, December 26, 2016. https:// www.cosmopolitan.com/career/a8526125/get-that-life-how-i- became-the-ceo-of-soulcycle/.

Spodek, Joshua. "Elite Universities Don't Get Failure." *Inc.Com*, June 30, 2017. https://www.inc.com/joshua-spodek/elite-uni- versities-failure-and-how-they-just-dont-.html.

Zenger, Jack. "The Confidence Gap in Men and Women: Why It Matters and How to Overcome It." *Forbes*, April 8, 2018. https://www.forbes.com/sites/jackzenger/2018/04/08/the-con- fidence-gap-in-men-and-women-why-it-matters-and-how-to- overcome-it/#7b12f9dc3bfa.

CHAPTER 2

Abrams, Abigail. "Yes, Impostor Syndrome Is Real. Here's How to Deal with It." *Time*, June 20, 2018. https://time.com/5312483/ how-to-deal-with-impostor-syndrome/.

Baer, Drake. "Here's Why Banning the Word 'Bossy' Is Great for Women." *Business Insider*, March 24, 2014. https://www.businessinsider.com/what-bossy-words-says-about-gender-at-work-2014-3.

Burn-Callander, Rebecca. "Why Imposter Syndrome Matters." *The Telegraph*, May 16, 2019. https://www.telegraph.co.uk/business/women-entrepreneurs/imposter-syndrome-women-careers/.

Chira, Susan. "Why Women Aren't C.E.O.S, According to Women Who Almost Were." *New York Times*, July 21, 2017. https://www.nytimes.com/2017/07/21/sunday-review/women-ceos-glass-ceiling.html.

Decker, Fred. "What Are the Qualifications to Be Listed as a Fortune 500 Company?" *Bizfluent*, October 22, 2018. https://bizfluent.com/list-6660518-qualifications-listed-fortune-500-company-.html.

Fuchs, Ken, dir. *The Bachelorette*. Season 15, episode 1, "Week 1: Season Premiere." Aired May 13, 2019, on ABC.

Hoff, Madison and Rachel Gillett. "Gender Bias Could Make It Harder for Women to Become CEO, According to a Recent Study." *Business Insider*, April 17, 2020. https://www.businessinsider.com/why-women-almost-never-become-ceo-2016-9.

Holmes, Michael. "Why Are There So Few Women CEOs?" *The Conversation*. https://theconversation.com/why-are-there-so-few-women-ceos-103212#:~:text=Unfortunately%2C%20many%20discriminatory%20factors%20reduce,are%20subject%20to%20gender%20stereotypes.&text=Regarding%20

supply%2Dside%20forces%2C%20there,family%20duties%20
than%20men%20do.

Page, Danielle. "How Impostor Syndrome Is Holding You Back
at Work." *Better by Today*, October 25, 2017. https://www.nbc-
news.com/better/health/how-impostor-syndrome-holding-
you-back-work-ncna814231.

Sandberg, Sheryl. *Lean In: Women, Work, and the Will to Lead.*
New York: Alfred A. Knopf, 2013.

Shapiro, Ari. "Why Major U.S. Companies Still Have So Few
Women CEOs." August 10, 2018. In *All Things Considered*.
Hosted by Ari Shapiro. Podcast. https://www.npr.org/2018/08/
10/637614737/why-major-u-s-companies-still-have-so-few-
women-ceos.

Trafford-Owens, Kirsty. "Women Are 'Bossy,' Men Are 'Leaders':
How Women in Power Are Perceived Differently to Men." *Druthers Search*, January 19, 2019. https://www.druthersearch.
com/2019-1-17-women-are-bossy-men-are-leaders-how-wom-
en-in-power-are-perceived-differently-to-men/.

Young, Valerie. *The Secret Thoughts of Successful Women: Why
Capable People Suffer from the Impostor Syndrome* and How to
Thrive in Spite of It. New York: Crown Business, 2011.

Zillman, Claire. "The Fortune 500 Has More Female CEOs
Than Ever Before." *Fortune*, May 16, 2019. https://fortune.
com/2019/05/16/fortune-500-female-ceos/.

CHAPTER 3

Broyles, Susannah. "Revolutionary Sisters: Victoria Woodhull and Tennessee Claflin." *MCNY Blog: New York Stories* (blog), June 24, 2014. https://blog.mcny.org/2014/06/24/revolutionary-sisters-victoria-woodhull-and-tennessee-claflin/.

Chapman, Lizette and Bloomberg. "Venture capital, long a boy's club, makes some progress in adding women." *Fortune*, February 7, 2020. https://fortune.com/2020/02/07/venture-capital-women-diversity/.

Contentworks Agency, "Women Who Rocked the Finance World— Muriel Faye 'Mickie' Siebert," *Medium*, April 2, 2019. https://medium.com/@contentworks/women-who-rocked-the-finance-world-muriel-faye-mickie-siebert-556800ddf2f8.

Contentworks Agency, "Women Who Rocked the Finance World— Rosemary McFadden," *Medium*, April 5, 2019. https://medium.com/@contentworks/women-who-rocked-the-finance-world-rosemary-mcfadden-33da7a3faaef.

Data USA. "Financial Managers." Accessed June 25, 2020. https://datausa.io/profile/soc/financial-managers.

Harris, Paige. "Women's History Month: Women in Finance," *Primeway* (blog). https://www.primewayfcu.com/blog/womens-history-month-women-in-finance.

Kapadia, Reshma. "Women in Finance Are Rising—at Last," *Barron's*, March 6, 2020. https://www.barrons.com/articles/women-are-advancing-to-senior-roles-in-u-s-financeslowly-51583436329.

Smith, Oliver. "30 Under 30 Europe: The Young Money Merchants Shaping Financial Markets In 2019." *Forbes*, February 12, 2019. https://www.forbes.com/sites/oliversmith/2019/02/12/30-under-30-europe-finance-the-young-money-merchants-shaping-financial-markets-in-2019/#383863462727.

The Venture Collective. "Our Past Investments." Accessed June 25, 2020.

"Women in Financial Services 2020." Oliver Wyman, 2020. https://www.oliverwyman.com/content/dam/oliver-wyman/v2/publications/2019/November/Women-In-Financial-Services-2020.pdf.

Young, Valerie. *The Secret Thoughts of Successful Women: Why Capable People Suffer from the Impostor Syndrome* and How to Thrive in Spite of It. New York: Crown Business, 2011.

CHAPTER 4

"5 Things to Do in Vegas If You Hate Vegas." BuzzFeed Video. March 18, 2019, Facebook, 2:49. https://www.facebook.com/buzzfeedbringme/videos/2619388664762612/?fallback=1.

"Grandmas Skydive for the First Time." BuzzFeed Video. May 2, 2015. YouTube video, 4:24. https://www.youtube.com/watch?v=50WtCQyMOrk.

LinkedIn. "Lizz Warner." Accessed October 7, 2020. https://www.linkedin.com/in/lizzwarner/.

Pantin, Laurence. "When Women Run Newsrooms, Women Are in the News." *We News*, April 6, 2001. https://womensenews.org/2001/04/when-women-run-newsrooms-women-are-the-news/.

Rhimes, Shonda. *Grey's Anatomy*. Season 12, episode 2, "Walking Tall." Aired October 1, 2015, on ABC.

Sandberg, Sheryl. *Lean In: Women, Work, and the Will to Lead*. New York: Alfred A. Knopf, 2013.

Stryker, Sam, Lizz Warner, and Kelly Diamond. "This Girl Matched on Tinder With an Olympic Athlete and Here's What Happened Next," BuzzFeed, April 7, 2018. https://www.buzzfeed.com/samstryker/olympics-tinder-date-sequel.

Women's Media Center. "The Status of Women in U.S. Media 2019." Accessed June 25, 2020. https://www.womensmediacenter.com/reports/the-status-of-women-in-u-s-media-2019.

Young, Valerie. *The Secret Thoughts of Successful Women: Why Capable People Suffer from the Impostor Syndrome* and How to Thrive in Spite of It. New York: Crown Business, 2011.

CHAPTER 5

Broadband Search. "Average Time Spent on Social Media (Latest 2020 Data)," https://www.broadbandsearch.net/blog/average-daily-time-on-social-media#:~:text=On%20average%2C%20we%20spend%20144,others%2C%20they%20spend%20far%20less.

BuzzFeed. "Ghosting." Accessed October 5, 2020. https://www.buzzfeed.com/tag/ghosting.

Herradura. "How Ella Mielniczenko's Journey Led Her to Become a Successful Executive Producer at BuzzFeed." *Forbes*, November 15, 2019. https://www.forbes.com/video/6103219397001/#6a1e32214df4.

Mirchevski, Bruno (HE). "An Interview with Ella Mielniczenko, Forbes (US & Canada 2019) Media," *Medium*, June 19, 2019. https://medium.com/the-logician/an-interview-with-ella-mielniczenko-forbes-us-canada-2019-media-e46020fe6d01.

TheBusinessQuotes.Com. "46 Knowledge-packed Mark Cuban quotes on how to stay in business." Accessed October 5, 2020.

Vukova, Christina. "73+ Surprising Networking Statistics to Boost Your Career." *Review42*, February 20, 2020. https://review42.com/networking-statistics/#:~:text=Statistics%20show%20that%2085%25%20of,least%20part%20of%20the%20time.&text=Considering%20what%20percentage%20of%20jobs,-likely%20be%20worth%20your%20time.

Young, Valerie. *The Secret Thoughts of Successful Women: Why Capable People Suffer from the Impostor Syndrome* and How to Thrive in Spite of It. New York: Crown Business, 2011.

YouTube. "BuzzFeed Violet." Accessed October 5, 2020. https://www.youtube.com/buzzfeedviolet.

YouTube. "BuzzFeed Violet Videos." Accessed October 5, 2020. https://www.youtube.com/c/buzzfeedviolet/videos.

YouTube. "Pero Like Videos." Accessed October 5, 2020. https://www.youtube.com/c/PeroLike/videos.

CHAPTER 6

Baker, Ashley. "Amy Odell Knows Why Your Digital Media Brand Is Failing," *The Daily Front Row*, February 12, 2018. https://fashionweekdaily.com/amy-odell/.

Odell, Amy. "My Job Interview with Anna Wintour." *New York Post*, August 30, 2015. https://nypost.com/2015/08/30/what-its-like-to-interview-with-anna-wintour/.

Petrarca, Emilia. "Cosmopolitan.com Editor Steps Down," *The Cut*, January 25, 2018. https://www.thecut.com/2018/01/cosmopolitan-editor-amy-odell-leaving.html.

Rudolph, Heather Wood. "Get That Life: How I Became the Editor of Cosmopolitan.com." August 31, 2015. https://www.cosmopolitan.com/career/interviews/a45511/get-that-life-amy-odell-cosmopolitan-tales-from-the-back-row/.

Tartakovsky, Margarita. "How Experts Achieve a Work-Life Balance and How

You Can Too," *PsychCentral*, October 8, 2018. https://psychcentral.com/lib/how-experts-achieve-a-work-life-balance-and-how-you-can-too/.

Young, Valerie. *The Secret Thoughts of Successful Women: Why Capable People Suffer from the Impostor Syndrome* and How to Thrive in Spite of It. New York: Crown Business, 2011.

CHAPTER 7

Bergelson Lab. "Elika Bergelson." Accessed July 5, 2020. https://bergelsonlab.com/bergelson-personal-page.html.

Bernstein, Rachel. "More female researchers globally, but challenges remain." *Sciencemag.org*, March 9, 2017. https://www.sciencemag.org/careers/2017/03/more-female-researchers-globally-challenges-remain.

Bey, Nadia. "Elika Bergelson wins early career award for child linguistic development research." *Duke Chronicle*, December 3, 2019. https://www.dukechronicle.com/article/2019/12/duke-university-bergelson-award-child-linguistic-development-research.

Boggs, Will. "Babies learn what words mean before they can use them." *Reuters*, November 20, 2017. https://fr.reuters.com/article/us-babies-language-idUSKBN1DK2FA.

Ducharme, Jamie. "Why It's So Hard to Learn Another Language after Childhood." *Time*, May 2, 2018. https://time.com/5261446/language-critical-period-age/.

Else, Holly. "Nearly half of US female scientists leave full-time science after first child." *Nature.com*, February 19, 2020. https://www.nature.com/articles/d41586-019-00611-1.

UNESCO, "Just 30% of the world's researchers are women. What's the situation in your country?" https://en.unesco.org/news/just-30-world%E2%80%99s-researchers-are-women-whats-situation-your-country.

Wall Street Journal. "ETrade 'Baby' Super Bowl Ad." February 1, 2013.

YouTube video, 0:18. https://www.youtube.com/watch?v=EbnWb-d9wSY.

Young, Valerie. *The Secret Thoughts of Successful Women: Why Capable People Suffer from the Impostor Syndrome* and How to Thrive in Spite of It. New York: Crown Business, 2011.

CHAPTER 8

Castrillon, Caroline. "How Introverts Can Thrive as Entrepreneurs." *Forbes*, January 23, 2019. https://www.forbes.com/sites/carolinecastrillon/2019/01/23/how-introverts-can-thrive-as-entrepreneurs/#5daf42005cac.

Horn, Brian Ainsley. "10 Quotes from Lori Greiner That Will Make You Proud to Be an Entrepreneur." *Authority Alchemy*.

Jamal, Sana. "21 million in Pakistan don't have access to clean water: report." *GulfNews*, March 22, 2018. https://gulfnews.com/world/asia/pakistan/21-million-in-pakistan-dont-have-access-to-clean-water-report-1.2192988#:~:text=Islamabad%3A%20Pakistan%20is%20one%20of,to%20mark%20World%20Water%20Day.

Krach, Keith. "10 of the Most Common Entrepreneurship Myths." *Medium.com*, May 23, 2017. https://medium.com/@Keith-Krach/10-of-the-most-common-entrepreneurship-myths-e241e51e9e2f.

Pandey, Kiran and Rajit Sengupta. "19% of world's people without access to clean water live in India." *DownToEarth*, March 23, 2018. https://www.downtoearth.org.in/news/water/19-of-worlds-people-without-access-to-clean-water-live-in-india-60011.

The Business Journals. "Arsheen Allam." https://profiles.bizjournals.com/profile/Arsheen-Allam-CEO-GOLeafe/851d164f-f11b-42af-b61e-21188f6c7132.

Warner, Christina. "Big Ideas with Founder and CEO of GOLeafe Arsheen Allam." *Thrive Global*, May 2, 2019. https://thriveglobal.com/stories/big-ideas-with-founder-and-ceo-of-cnanoz-inc-arsheen-allam/.

CHAPTER 9

Agnihotri, Deepti. "Alumni Profile: Megan O'Connor." Duke Civil & Environmental Engineering, April 25, 2018. https://cee.duke.edu/about/news/alumni-profile-megan-oconnor.

Investments Masters Class. "What You Know?" Accessed May 20, 2020. http://mastersinvest.com/whatyouknowquotes.

LinkedIn. "Innovations Crossroads." Accessed May 15, 2020. https://www.linkedin.com/company/innovation-crossroads/.

Murray, Seb. "Women Business Leaders Do It Better Without MBAs – Fortune." *BusinessBecause*, September 22, 2014. https://www.businessbecause.com/news/other-masters/2797/women-business-leaders-do- it-better-without-mbas.

Nth Cycle. "About Nth Cycle." Accessed May 15, 2020. https://www.nthcycle.com/about.

Oppong, Thomas. "49 Ways to Become a Better Entrepreneur." LinkedIn, October 30, 2018. https://www.linkedin.com/pulse/49-ways-become-better-entrepreneur-thomas-oppong/.

Rasmussen, Dan & Haonan Li. "The MBA Myth and the Cult of the CEO." *Institutional Investor*, February 27, 2019. https://www.institutionalinvestor.com/article/b1db3jy3201d38/The-MBA-Myth-and-the-Cult-of-the-CEO.

The World Counts. "Electronic Revolution=E-Waste." Accessed May 15, 2020. https://www.theworldcounts.com/stories/Electronic-Waste-Facts.

Young, Valerie. *The Secret Thoughts of Successful Women: Why Capable People Suffer from the Impostor Syndrome* and How to Thrive in Spite of It. New York: Crown Business, 2011.

CHAPTER 10

Baliunaite, Ilona. "30 Alarming Posts about How the Student Debt System Affects People's Lives and It's Terrible." *Bored Panda*. https://www.boredpanda.com/student-debt-crisis-posts/?utm_source=google&utm_medium=organic&utm_campaign=organic.

Bumble. "Spotlight: Charlie Javice of Frank." Accessed July 5, 2020. https://bumble.com/the-buzz/working-title.

Burnett, Mark, dir. *Shark Tank*, Season 4 episode 1, "Episode 401." Aired September 4, 2012, on ABC.

Frank. "How It Works." Accessed May 25, 2020. https://withfrank. org/how-it-works/?_ga=2.258010184.338384037.1600837354-281970605.1600837353.

Haselton, Jessica. "Investing in Women-Led Edtech Startups Is More Than a Matter of Equity. It's Also Good Business." *EdSurge*, February 12, 2020. https://www.edsurge.com/ news/2020-02-12-investing-in-women-led-edtech-startups-is-more-than-a-matter-of-equity-it-s-also-good-business.

Hassler, Chelsea Adelaine. "How a 25-Year-Old Woman Is Rebuilding the College Financial Aid Process, 1 Student at a Time." *Pop Sugar*, January 22, 2018. https://www.popsugar. com/news/Frank-FAFSA-Founder-CEO-Charlie-Javice-Interview-44518650.

Hess, Abigail. "Fewer than 1 in 5 Americans think the college admissions process is fair." *CNBC*, March 20, 2019. https:// www.cnbc.com/2019/03/20/under-20percent-of-americans-think-the-college admissions-process-is-fair.html.

Hutto, Cara. "Meet the Woman Making Quality Education Affordable for All." *Women to Know (blog)*, *In Her Sight*, September 22, 2018. https://www.inhersight.com/blog/working-women/ charlie-javice-frank-enabling-afford-colleg?_n=130998111.

Johnston, Andy. "One surprising barrier to college success: Dense higher education lingo." *Heching Report*, June 14, 2019. https://

hechingerreport.org/one-surprising-barrier-to-success-in-college-understanding-higher-education-lingo/.

Long, Bridget Terry, Judith Scott-Clayton, Kim Cook, and Kristin Hultquist. "FAFSA: Ask any college student. The federal student aid application is needlessly complex." *USA Today*, December 9, 2019. https://www.usatoday.com/story/opinion/2019/12/05/fafsa-ask-any-college-student-federal-student-aid-application-column/2598151001/.

Mohan, Pavithra. "This is what women endure when trying to raise capital." *Fast Company*, September 18, 2018. https://www.fastcompany.com/90235052/this-is-what-women-endure-when-trying-to-raise-capital.

Wan, Tony. "Is Education Technology Where Women Are Starting to Buck the Tech World's Sexist Trends?" *Fast Company*, April 4, 2015. https://www.fastcompany.com/3043779/is-education-technology-where-women-are-starting-to-buck-the-tech-world.

Wilhelm, Alex. "Frank raises $5M more in its quest to get students max financial aid." *Tech Crunch*, April 13, 2020. https://techcrunch.com/2020/04/13/frank-raises-5m-more-in-its-quest-to-get-students-max-financial-aid/?guce_referrer=aHR0cHM6Ly9xdWlwLmNvbS88&guce_referrer_sig=AQAAANB5SRWaLkl_NQnWhBtuXturslZbe-YPPBZ-vBWwq1xK_fxf_5EtOj1vqL4zh5SooMURL4a8qYWOvdvVER-aSjKFHAbvl_jIZMU6RNQ5oWiO4jSkEnYTBiUbwUhdG8cS-rqzKdsV6JS-GPp9M8aRuqGQ_3EYtB63BXx-puD33HIuIxk&-guccounter=2.

Young, Valerie. *The Secret Thoughts of Successful Women: Why Capable People Suffer from the Impostor Syndrome* and How to Thrive in Spite of It. New York: Crown Business, 2011.

CHAPTER 11

Code.org. "About Us." Accessed May 6, 2020. https://code.org/about.

Code.org. "More Data and Talking Points for Advocacy." Accessed May 6, 2020. https://code.org/promote/morestats.

Google. "Computer Science Learning: Closing the Gap: Girls." Accessed May 5, 2020. http://services.google.com/fh/files/misc/computer-science-learning-closing-the-gap-girls-brief.pdf.

"Quotes about Recognizing your Network." *Ellevate.* https://www.ellevatenetwork.com/articles/8383-quotes-about-recognizing-your-network.

Vukova, Christina. "73+ Surprising Networking Statistics to Boost Your Career." *Review 42*, February 20, 2020. https://review42.com/networking-statistics/.

Young, Valerie. *The Secret Thoughts of Successful Women: Why Capable People Suffer from the Impostor Syndrome* and How to Thrive in Spite of It. New York: Crown Business, 2011.

CHAPTER 12

Adtlive.com, "About." Accessed October 5, 2020. http://www.atdlive.com/.

Day, Anna Therese. "Dining with Al Qaeda." *The Daily Beast*, July 11, 2017. https://www.thedailybeast.com/dining-with-al-qaeda.

"Egypt Revolution: 18 days of people power." *Al Jazeera*, January 25, 2016. https://www.aljazeera.com/gallery/2016/1/25/egypt-revolution-18-days-of-people-power/.

Goudreau, Jenna. "Mark Cuban Reveals the Best and Worst 'Shark Tank' Pitches and More," *Business Insider*, November 11, 2013. https://www.businessinsider.com/mark-cuban-reveals-best-and-worst-shark-tank-pitches-2013-11.

International Women's Media Foundation. "19 women changing journalism in 2019." Accessed October 5, 2020. https://www.iwmf.org/19-women-who-shaped-the-future-of-journalism-in-2019/.

York, Catherine. "Women dominate journalism schools, but newsrooms are still a different story." *Poynter*, September 18, 2017. https://www.poynter.org/business-work/2017/women-dominate-journalism-schools-but-newsrooms-are-still-a-different-story/.

Young, Valerie. *The Secret Thoughts of Successful Women: Why Capable People Suffer from the Impostor Syndrome* and How to Thrive in Spite of It. New York: Crown Business, 2011.

CHAPTER 13

Nuamah, Sally A. "On the International Day of the Girl, it's a good time to ask: are girls safe in school?" *The Washington Post*, October 11, 2018. https://www.washingtonopst.com/news/

monkey-cage-wp/2018/10/11/on-the-international-day-of-the-girl-its-a-good-time-to-ask-are-girls-safe-in-schools.

Pousoulides, Stefanie. "Sally Nuamah on how punishment against black girls impacts our democracy," *The Chronicle*, August 8, 2019. https://www.dukechronicle.com/article/2019/08/sally-nuamah-punishment-against-black-girls-impacts-democracy-duke-northwestern.

SallyNuamah.com, "Short Bio." Accessed October 7, 2020. http://www.sallynuamah.com/about.

TEDx Talks, "Clapping with One Hand: Sally Nuamah at TEDx-UofIChicago." May 3, 2013, video, 11:46. https://www.youtube.com/watch?v=2cgUvqc-GKc.

Young, Valerie. *The Secret Thoughts of Successful Women: Why Capable People Suffer from the Impostor Syndrome* and How to Thrive in Spite of It. New York: Crown Business, 2011.

CHAPTER 14

Apple Tree Partners. "Approach." Accessed September 30, 2020. https://www.appletreepartners.com/approach.

Boulder Care. "About Boulder Care." Accessed September 30, 2020. https://boulder.care/about.

Boulder Care. Facebook. https://www.facebook.com/pg/Boulder-Care/posts/?ref=page_internal.

Coward, Kyle. "Boulder Care Announces $10.5M in Series A Funding." *Behavioral Health Business*, February 14, 2020. https://bhbusiness.com/2020/02/14/boulder-care-announces-10-5m-in-series-a-funding/.

LinkedIn. "Stephanie (Papes) Strong." Accessed September 28, 2020. https://www.linkedin.com/in/stephaniepapes/.

Nana Wilson, PhD; Mbabazi Kariisa, PhD; Puja Seth, PhD; Herschel Smith IV, MPH; Nicole L. Davis, PhD, "Drug and Opioid-Involved Overdose Deaths—United States, 2017–2018." CDC, March 20, 2020. https://www.cdc.gov/mmwr/volumes/69/wr/mm6911a4.htm.

Papes, Stephanie. "We know how to treat opiate addiction: now we must get care to patients." *Medium*, March 13, 2018. https://medium.com/@HealthyDialog/we-already-know-how-to-treat-addiction-now-we-must-get-care-to-patients-34ef1ef15388.

Sainato, Michael. "The Americans dying because they can't afford medical care." *The Guardian*, January 7, 2020. https://www.theguardian.com/us-news/2020/jan/07/americans-health-care-medical-costs.

Thomas Jefferson University Online. "Exploring Gender Bias in Healthcare." *MedCityNews*, September 4, 2019. https://medcitynews.com/?sponsored_content=exploring-gender-bias-in-healthcare.

Young, Valerie. *The Secret Thoughts of Successful Women: Why Capable People Suffer from the Impostor Syndrome* and How to Thrive in Spite of It. New York: Crown Business, 2011.

CHAPTER 15

Elven, Marjorie van. "Why is it so hard for women to become CEOs in fashion companies?" *Fashion United,* May 8, 2019. https://au.fashionunited.com/news/business/why-is-it-so-hard-for-women-to-become-ceos-in-apparel-companies/201905088446.

Fair Harbor. "About Us." Accessed July 15, 2020. https://www.fair-harborclothing.com/pages/about.

"Fair Harbor." *Forbes.* Accessed July 16, 2020. https://www.forbes.com/profile/fair-harbor/#1736ba243ef7.

Milnes, Hilary. "When female fashion founders meet mansplaining VCs." *Glossy.com*, September 29, 2016. https://www.glossy.co/ecommerce/how-fashion-startups-get-funding-in-a-male-dominated-vc-industry.

Phillips, Robert. "Why do so few university graduates start their own businesses?" *The Guardian*, December 14, 2018. https://www.theguardian.com/education/2018/dec/14/why-do-so-few-university-graduates-start-their-own-businesses.

Weiner, Yitzi. "Know the Importance of Bootstrapping' 5 Startup Strategies with Caroline Danehy, Co-Founder of Fair Harbor Clothing," *Thrive Global*, February 26, 2018. https://medium.com/thrive-global/know-the-the-importance-of-bootstrapping-5-startup-strategies-with-caroline-danehy-co-founder-of-af900e90b4cf.

Young, Valerie. *The Secret Thoughts of Successful Women: Why Capable People Suffer from the Impostor Syndrome* and How to Thrive in Spite of It. New York: Crown Business, 2011.

CHAPTER 16

Bajkowski, Jared. "Meet the Hallmark social media pro who just made Forbes' 30 Under 30 list." *The Kansas City Star*, November 30, 2017. https://www.kansascity.com/article187303998.html.

Baumgartner, Jeffrey. "When you Need Breakthrough Ideas, Consider Anti-conventional Thinking," *Innovation Management*. https://innovationmanagement.se/2011/05/11/when-you-need-breakthrough-ideas-consider-anti-conventional-thinking/.

Bikker, Yannick. "You're Not You When You're Hungry: The Best Ad Campaign Ever?" *Medium*, March 21, 2020. https://medium.com/better-marketing/youre-not-you-when-you-re-hungry-the-best-ad-campaign-ever-4a46c59a4b13.

Edelman. "HP #MoreLikeMe." Accessed September 25, 2020. https://www.edelman.com/work/hp-more-like-me.

Liffreing, Ilyse. "Facebook is hosting 'Cannected' events around the world for creatives who can't make it to Cannes Lions." *Campaign Live*, June 14, 2017. https://www.campaignlive.com/article/facebook-hosting-cannected-events-around-world-creatives-cant-cannes-lions/1436545.

LinkedIn. "Arielle Gross Samuels." Accessed September 15, 2020.

LinkedIn. "Thea Neal." Accessed September 15, 2020. https://www.linkedin.com/in/nealthea/.

LMA. "Wendy's Is Roasting People on Twitter, and It's Just Too Funny." *Bored Panda*. https://www.boredpanda.com/funny-wendy-jokes/?utm_source=google&utm_medium=organic&utm_campaign=organic.

Neal, Thea. "Imposter Syndrome, or what I faced after being named to Forbes 30 Under 30." *LinkedIn*, November 27, 2017. https://www.linkedin.com/pulse/imposter-syndrome-what-i-faced-after-being-named-forbes-thea-neal/.

Rooney, Jenny. "The World's Most Influential CMOs 2019." *Forbes*, June 20, 2019. https://www.forbes.com/sites/jenniferrooney/2019/06/20/the-worlds-most-influential-cmos-2019/#61ceaf523d3c.

State Farm Insurance. "Back in the Office | State Farm'." YouTube video. https://www.youtube.com/watch?v=tEaTrmlZUgw.

Taylor, Kate. "Wendy's jumps into the chicken-sandwich Twitter feud between Popeyes and Chick-fil-A." *Business Insider*, August 20, 2019. https://www.businessinsider.com/wendys-enters-popeyes-chick-fil-a-chicken-sandwich-battle-2019-8.

"Thea Neal." *Forbes*. Accessed September 15, 2020. https://www.forbes.com/pictures/59fa3fbaa7ea436b47b4ba6a/thea-neal-29/#56073e0d2aa7.

"Understanding Impressions in digital marketing," Big Commerce, accessed September 16, 2020. https://www.bigcommerce.com/ecommerce-answers/impressions-digital-marketing/#:~:text=Definition%3A%20Impressions%20are%20when%20an,intent%20on%20spreading%20brand%20awareness.

Young, Valerie. *The Secret Thoughts of Successful Women: Why Capable People Suffer from the Impostor Syndrome* and How to Thrive in Spite of It. New York: Crown Business, 2011.

CHAPTER 17

Luketic, Robert, dir. *Legally Blonde.* 2001; Beverly Hills, CA: Metro-Goldwyn-Mayer. DVD.

Goodreads.com, "The Secret Thoughts of Successful Women." Accessed October 11, 2020. https://www.goodreads.com/book/show/10878510-the-secret-thoughts-of-successful-women.

Wilding, Melody. "5 Different Types of Imposter Syndrome (and 5 Ways to Battle Each One," *The Muse.* https://www.themuse.com/advice/5-different-types-of-imposter-syndrome-and-5-ways-to-battle-each-one.

Young, Valerie. *The Secret Thoughts of Successful Women: Why Capable People Suffer from the Impostor Syndrome* and How to Thrive in Spite of It. New York: Crown Business, 2011.

CPSIA information can be obtained
at www.ICGtesting.com
Printed in the USA
BVHW091124301220
596710BV00005B/13